S. Hrg. 113–482

FISHERIES TREATIES AND PORT STATE MEASURES AGREEMENTS

HEARING

BEFORE THE

COMMITTEE ON FOREIGN RELATIONS
UNITED STATES SENATE

ONE HUNDRED THIRTEENTH CONGRESS

SECOND SESSION

FEBRUARY 12, 2014

Printed for the use of the Committee on Foreign Relations

Available via the World Wide Web: http://www.gpo.gov/fdsys/

U.S. GOVERNMENT PRINTING OFFICE

91–389 PDF WASHINGTON : 2014

For sale by the Superintendent of Documents, U.S. Government Printing Office
Internet: bookstore.gpo.gov Phone: toll free (866) 512–1800; DC area (202) 512–1800
Fax: (202) 512–2104 Mail: Stop IDCC, Washington, DC 20402–0001

COMMITTEE ON FOREIGN RELATIONS

ROBERT MENENDEZ, New Jersey, *Chairman*

BARBARA BOXER, California
BENJAMIN L. CARDIN, Maryland
JEANNE SHAHEEN, New Hampshire
CHRISTOPHER A. COONS, Delaware
RICHARD J. DURBIN, Illinois
TOM UDALL, New Mexico
CHRISTOPHER MURPHY, Connecticut
TIM KAINE, Virginia
EDWARD J. MARKEY, Massachusetts

BOB CORKER, Tennessee
JAMES E. RISCH, Idaho
MARCO RUBIO, Florida
RON JOHNSON, Wisconsin
JEFF FLAKE, Arizona
JOHN McCAIN, Arizona
JOHN BARRASSO, Wyoming
RAND PAUL, Kentucky

DANIEL E. O'BRIEN, *Staff Director*
LESTER E. MUNSON III, *Republican Staff Director*

(II)

CONTENTS

Page

Balton, Hon. David A., Deputy Assistant Secretary for Oceans and Fisheries, Bureau of Oceans and International Environmental and Scientific Affairs, U.S. Department of State, Washington, DC 6
    Prepared statement 8
Gleason, Mark, Executive Director, Alaska Bering Sea Crabbers, Seattle, WA 37
    Prepared statement 39
Kane, Raymond, Outreach Coordinator, Cape Cod Fishermen's Alliance, Chatham, MA 28
    Prepared statement 30
Kenney, Hon. Admiral Frederick J., Judge Advocate General and Chief Counsel, U.S. Coast Guard, Washington, DC 23
    Prepared statement 25
Lagon, Hon. Mark P., Global Politics and Security Chair, Master of Science in Foreign Service Program, Georgetown University, and Adjunct Senior Fellow for Human Rights, Council on Foreign Relations, Washington, DC 31
    Prepared statement 33
Markey, Hon. Edward J., U.S. Senator From Massachusetts, opening statement 1
Murkowski, Hon. Lisa, U.S. Senator From Alaska 20
    Prepared statement 22
Smith, Russell F. III, Deputy Assistant Secretary for International Fisheries, National Oceanic and Atmospheric Administration, U.S. Department of Commerce, Washington, DC 12
    Prepared statement 13
Whitehouse, Hon. Sheldon, U.S. Senator From Rhode Island 3
    Prepared statement 4

ADDITIONAL MATERIAL SUBMITTED FOR THE RECORD

Response of Deputy Assistant Secretary David Balton to Question Submitted by Senator Robert Menendez 43
Responses of Russell Smith III to Questions Submitted by Senator Marco Rubio 45
Responses of Adm. Frederick J. Kenney to Questions Submitted by Senator Marco Rubio 46
Responses of Ambassador Mark Lagon to Questions Submitted by Senator Marco Rubio 47
Letter Submitted on Behalf of the Federal Law Enforcement Officers Association 50
Letter Submitted on Behalf of the Joint Ocean Commission Initiative 52
Letter Submitted on Behalf of Various Stakeholders Urging Ratification of the Treaties 54

FISHERIES TREATIES AND PORT STATE MEASURES AGREEMENTS

WEDNESDAY, FEBRUARY 12, 2014

U.S. SENATE,
COMMITTEE ON FOREIGN RELATIONS,
Washington, DC

The committee met, pursuant to notice, at 2:38 p.m., in room SD–419, Dirksen Senate Office Building, Hon. Edward J. Markey presiding.

Present: Senators Markey and Rubio.

OPENING STATEMENT OF HON. EDWARD J. MARKEY, U.S. SENATOR FROM MASSACHUSETTS

Senator MARKEY. Welcome. Good afternoon. The committee will come to order. Today we will hear testimony on the Port State Measures Agreement and three regional fishing management organization agreements. All of them will help combat illegal fishing and improve the management of fisheries in international waters, to the benefit of U.S. fishermen, our seafood industry, and U.S. security interests.

The ocean is vast. From the land it is hard to contemplate its limits or how illegal fishing in distant waters might impact the United States. But like dropping a pebble in a pond, the ripple effects of illegal fishing expand to all shores. The impact of illegal fishing has already reached Cape Cod and the ports of New England, where commercial fishing has been the lifeblood of communities for centuries. Our small boat fishermen have always supplemented their cod catches with a variety of fish. Bluefin tuna and swordfish have been especially important. Landing one can mean the difference between a profitable fishing season or not, between the paying of the mortgage on time or not, between helping with a daughter's college bills or not. With our cod stocks struggling and facing the ongoing impacts of climate change, revenue from other fish becomes even more important.

But there is not enough American tuna or European tuna or African tuna. There is Atlantic tuna, and what happens in the Atlantic beyond any country's control can impact fishermen in every country.

Today we will hear from a 40-year fishing veteran, Captain Ray Kane, about how illegal fishing far from our shores has an impact on the fishing lines and business bottom lines of the fishermen from his home port of Chatham, MA, and across New England.

But this is not just an Atlantic problem. We will also hear about the challenges facing American crabbers in the Bering Sea. And it

(1)

is not just American fishermen that suffer. If you watched the recent movie "Captain Phillips" about the Somali pirates hijacking the *Maersk Alabama* in 2009, you heard the pirates' leader mention foreign vessels taking away the Somali fish. As Somalia descended into chaos in the 1990s, they lost the ability to police their national waters. Foreign vessels moved in and depleted fish stocks that helped support coastal communities, increasing the incentive for Somalis to take up piracy.

Sadly, their story has now come full circle. As the United States and our allies have increased efforts to protect shipping off the Horn of Africa, Somali pirates are now providing protection to the vessels engaged in illegal fishing. Of course, unscrupulous captains willing to harvest fish illegally are also willing to partake in other illegal activities.

We will also hear testimony today about the connection between illegal fishing and human trafficking.

The high seas will never be 100 percent secure, but the agreements that are the subject of this hearing will help. A fish is worthless unless it is sold at a dock. The Port State Measures Agreement will shrink the number of ports where illegal fishing boats can find safe harbor and the economic incentive to engage in illegal fishing. It will bring the rest of the world up to the standards of the United States and ensure fairness for our fishermen in the global market.

The other three agreements will create and strengthen the rules for fishing in international waters that will improve conservation efforts and support sustainable management of important fish stocks.

Our domestic fishermen are the first to feel the impacts of illegal fishing, both from reduction in fish to catch and reduction in the price they get when they can take fish to market. But illegal fishing and seafood fraud ripples through the entire seafood industry, from processors to restaurant owners to seafood lovers looking for a delicious meal.

That is why organizations from the National Fisheries Institute to the Federal Law Enforcement Officers Association to conservation groups have written in support of the agreements we have before us today. I ask that these letters and statements be included in the record.

Today's four agreements are important. I look forward to working with Chairman Menendez and Ranking Member Corker to move these through our committee quickly, to benefit our American fishermen and the seafood industry. U.S. fishery management is the most rigorous in the world. Our domestic laws already accomplish much of what is required under these agreements. But I look forward to working with my colleagues on the Commerce Committee to move any additional legislation necessary to ensure the full participation of the United States.

Because of the rollcall confusion on the Senate floor at this particular point in time, Senator Rubio is a little bit delayed and requests that we proceed without him, and we will continue this hearing, although there are at least six additional rollcalls that are pending on the Senate floor.

So bear with us in the course of this afternoon.

Our first witness, Senator Sheldon Whitehouse from Rhode Island, is one of the cochairs of the Senate Ocean Caucus along with Senator Murkowski, and he has been working to educate the Senate and the public about the importance of these agreements that come before the committee today. We welcome you, Senator Whitehouse. Whenever you are ready, please begin.

STATEMENT OF HON. SHELDON WHITEHOUSE, U.S. SENATOR FROM RHODE ISLAND

Senator WHITEHOUSE. Thank you, Senator Markey, for having me here this afternoon for this hearing on international fisheries. As you mentioned, I serve as a cochair of the Senate Oceans Caucus along with my colleague, Senator Murkowski. For similar reasons to those that detain Senator Rubio, she is not here presently either, and I ask unanimous consent that whatever statement she may submit be incorporated into the record as if she were here with me now.

Senator MARKEY. Without objection, so ordered.

Senator WHITEHOUSE. She and Senator Begich and Senator Wicker are the four cochairs of our Senate Oceans Caucus, which works to find bipartisan common ground on issues that affect our oceans and coasts. One area that we all agree deserves our attention is illegal, unregulated, and unreported fishing, commonly referred to as ''pirate fishing.''

The work of our caucus on this issue builds on the bipartisan tradition in the Senate of support for international fisheries management. Since the 1950s, the Senate has ratified at least 15 international fisheries treaties with bipartisan support, not to mention additional amendments to existing treaties.

Fishing industries, as the Senator from Massachusetts well knows, are integral to coastal economies. Indeed, in 2011 U.S. commercial fish landings generated $5.3 billion and recreational anglers spent $26.8 billion.

At the same time, however, we are seeing estimated worldwide losses due to pirate fishing between 10 and $23.5 billion annually. Pirate fishing puts fishermen and processors in our home States who are playing by the rules at an unfair disadvantage. Pirate fishing is conducted outside laws that protect the fishery, and by cheating they can operate at a lower cost and undercut the prices U.S. fishermen must set following the rules.

The problem is not just local. Fish migrate. Pirate fishing in foreign countries, on the high seas, and of course in our own backyard, can jeopardize migratory fish stocks that our domestic fishermen rely on. Quite simply, this is a problem we cannot afford to ignore.

The agreement on Port State Measures to prevent, deter, and eliminate illegal, unreported, and unregulated fishing was adopted in response to this issue. It will allow the United States and other countries to bar pirate fishing vessels from entering ports and bringing their goods to market. Information-sharing networks to track offenders and a compliance structure are also established under the agreement.

The agreement has strong support outside of this Chamber. Here is what Chris Lischewski, President and CEO of Bumble Bee

Foods, has said, ''IUU fishing is a multibillion dollar industry that undermines our global conservation and sustainability efforts. Illegal fishing penalizes legitimate fishermen and processors and it must be stopped. While the United States has done a good job at developing laws to detect and deter IUU fishing, other nations have not. We strongly support the agreement on Port State Measures to prevent, deter, and eliminate illegal, unreported, and unregulated fishing because it creates an obligation for other nations to take action against IUU fishing.''

That is the President of Bumble Bee Foods.

Literally billions of dollars that could have gone into the hands of law-abiding fishermen and responsible seafood companies are lost every year. The Port State Measures Agreement gives us and others new tools to stop this thievery.

Three other treaty documents have also been received in the Senate during the 113th Congress relating to high seas fisheries. Fair control measures and enforcement at this scale allows us to protect our fishermen by ensuring the longevity of the fish stocks on which they depend.

The United States includes over 4 million square miles of the Pacific, Atlantic, and Arctic Oceans, the Gulf of Mexico, and the Caribbean Sea. Our fishermen and their industry partners can benefit from well-managed resources. Bill Ruckelshaus and Norm Mineta, both previously high-level political appointees in Republican and Democratic administrations respectively, cochair the Joint Ocean Commission Initiative. They offer this thought in a letter that I would like to submit for the record: ''Sustainable management of our ocean resources for current and future generations requires an international framework and a consistently applied rule of law across nations. Ratification of these treaties taken as a whole is an important step in this direction and helps affirm the role of the United States as a leader in protecting our global commons for the benefit and use of our citizens.''

Senator WHITEHOUSE. As cochairs of the Senate Oceans Caucus, Senator Murkowski and I express bipartisan support for the four pending international fisheries management treaties. We are now collecting signatures on a letter of support to Senate leadership. The Senate should ratify these treaties, which are supported by the Alaska Bering Sea Crabbers, National Fisheries Institute, Ocean Champions, World Wildlife Fund, Pew Charitable Trusts, and Environmental Defense Fund, among others.

I thank you, chairman, for entertaining my thoughts here today.

[The prepared statement of Senator Whitehouse follows:]

PREPARED STATEMENT OF SENATOR SHELDON WHITEHOUSE

Thank you Senator Markey, Chairman Menendez, and Ranking Member Corker, for having me this afternoon and for holding this hearing on international fisheries. I am privileged to serve, along with Senators Murkowski, Begich, and Wicker, as a cochair of the Senate Oceans Caucus, which works to find bipartisan common ground on issues affecting our oceans and coasts, and the people and communities that rely on them.

One area we all agree deserves our attention is illegal, unregulated, and unreported fishing; commonly referred to as pirate fishing. The work of our Caucus on this issue builds on the bipartisan tradition in the Senate of support for international fisheries management. Since the 1950s, the Senate has ratified at least 15 international fisheries treaties with bipartisan support, not to mention additional amendments to existing treaties.

Fishing industries are integral to coastal economies. Indeed, in 2011, U.S. commercial fish landings generated $5.3 billion and recreational anglers spent $26.8 billion. At the same time, however, we are seeing estimated worldwide losses due to pirate fishing between $10 and $23.5 billion annually.

Pirate fishing puts fishermen and processors in our home States who are playing by the rules at an unfair disadvantage. Pirate fishing is conducted outside laws that protect the fishery, and by cheating they can operate at a lower cost and undercut the prices U.S. fishermen must set following the rules.

The problem isn't just local. Fish migrate. Pirate fishing in foreign countries, on the high seas, and even in our own backyard can jeopardize migratory fish stocks that our domestic fishermen rely on.

Quite simply, this is a problem we can't afford to ignore.

The "Agreement on Port State Measures to Prevent, Deter and Eliminate Illegal, Unreported and Unregulated Fishing" was adopted in response to this issue. It will allow the U.S. and other countries to bar pirate fishing vessels from entering ports and bringing their goods to market. Information-sharing networks to track offenders and a compliance structure are also established under the agreement.

The agreement has strong support outside of this chamber. Here's what Chris Lischewski, CEO and President of Bumble Bee Foods, has said: "IUU fishing is a multibillion dollar industry that undermines our global conservation and sustainability efforts. Illegal fishing penalizes legitimate fishermen and processors and it must be stopped. While the United States has done a good job at developing laws to detect and deter IUU fishing, other nations have not. We strongly support the 'Agreement on Port State Measures to Prevent, Deter, and Eliminate Illegal, Unreported, and Unregulated Fishing' because it creates an obligation for other nations to take action against IUU fishing."

Literally billions of dollars that could have gone into the hands of law-abiding fishermen and responsible seafood companies are lost every year. The Port States Measures Agreement gives us and others new tools to stop this thievery.

Three other treaty documents have also been received in the Senate during the 113th Congress relating to managing high seas fisheries. Fair control measures and enforcement at this scale allows us to protect our fishermen by ensuring the longevity of fish stocks.

The United States includes over 4 million square miles of the Pacific, Atlantic, and Arctic Oceans, the Gulf of Mexico, and the Caribbean Sea. Our fishermen and their industry partners can benefit from well-managed resources.

Bill Ruckelshaus and Norm Mineta, both previously high-level political appointees in Republican and Democratic administrations respectively, cochair the Joint Ocean Commission Initiative. They offer this thought in a letter I would like to submit for the record: "Sustainable management of our ocean resources for current and future generations requires an international framework and a consistently applied rule of law across nations. Ratification of these treaties, taken as a whole, is an important step in this direction and helps affirm the role of the United States as a leader in protecting our global commons for the benefit and use of our citizens."

As cochairs of the Senate Oceans Caucus we express bipartisan support for the four pending international fisheries management treaties. We are now collecting signatures on a letter of support to Senate leadership.

The Senate should ratify these treaties, which are supported by the Alaska Bering Sea Crabbers, National Fisheries Institute, Ocean Champions, World Wildlife Fund, The Pew Charitable Trusts, and Environmental Defense Fund.

Senator MARKEY. Thank you, Senator, very much, and thank you for the organizing around this very important issue which you are leading. We thank you and we thank Senator Murkowski.

Now we are going to turn to our second panel: the Honorable David Balton, Mr. Russell Smith, and Rear Admiral Frederick Kenney. If you could each come up and sit at the panel, we can begin.

[Pause.]

Senator MARKEY. I would like to thank the witnesses and their colleagues for their hard work in bringing the agreements before us today. I will briefly introduce them all and then we can hear their testimony.

Our first witness is Ambassador David Balton. He is the Deputy Assistant Secretary for Oceans and Fisheries in the Bureau of Oceans and International Environmental and Scientific Affairs at the U.S. Department of State. He has served in that position since February of 2009.

Our second witness is Russell Smith. He is the Deputy Assistant Secretary for International Fisheries at the National Oceanic and Atmospheric Administration. He is currently serving as the Acting United States Federal Commissioner for both the Western and Central Pacific Fisheries Commissions and the International Convention for the Conservation of Atlantic Tunas.

Our third witness is Rear Admiral Frederick J. Kenney. He is the Judge Advocate General and Chief Counsel of the Coast Guard. His responsibilities include delivering legal services in support of Coast Guard missions.

Ambassador Balton, we will begin with you and then we will go down the table in the order of the seating arrangement. So welcome, sir. Whenever you feel comfortable, please begin.

STATEMENT OF HON. DAVID A. BALTON, DEPUTY ASSISTANT SECRETARY FOR OCEANS AND FISHERIES, BUREAU OF OCEANS AND INTERNATIONAL ENVIRONMENTAL AND SCIENTIFIC AFFAIRS, U.S. DEPARTMENT OF STATE, WASHINGTON, DC

Ambassador BALTON. Thank you very much, Mr. Chairman. I am pleased to testify today in support of the four international fisheries agreements pending before the committee. With your permission, I would like my written statement submitted for the record.

Senator MARKEY. Without objection, so ordered.

Ambassador BALTON. These four agreements address critical fisheries resources. Two new regional agreements cover high seas fisheries in the North Pacific and South Pacific Oceans respectively. The third agreement amends a treaty that created the Northwest Atlantic Fisheries Organization, of which the United States is already a member. The fourth agreement, on Port State Measures, is global in nature and, as you said, it addresses what is commonly referred to as pirate fishing or illegal, unreported, and unregulated fishing.

We commend the committee for considering these agreements. U.S. ratification will allow our Nation to reinforce its leadership role on oceans issues and to advance U.S. interests in marine fisheries. Each of these agreements has strong support from a broad range of stakeholders, including the U.S. fishing industry, the environmental and scientific communities. Representatives of these communities participated actively in the negotiations of these agreements. Let me say just a word or two about each of them.

The first agreement—and I think you will see a chart on the easel there—is the Convention on Fisheries Resources of the North Pacific Ocean. This treaty will establish the North Pacific Fisheries Commission, through which parties will cooperate to manage fisheries across an enormous expanse of high seas in the North Pacific Ocean. This area includes areas immediately adjacent to the U.S.

Exclusive Economic Zone off Alaska, the Pacific West Coast, Hawaii, and other U.S. territories and possessions in the North Pacific.

U.S. ratification would give the United States a strong voice in managing fishing activities just outside the U.S. EEZ that could have a direct impact on resources within our EEZ. Ratification will also ensure that U.S. vessels will have a legitimate right to participate in fisheries in this area.

The second agreement covers high seas fisheries resources in the South Pacific region. The high seas areas covered here are near American Samoa and a number of other U.S. islands in this part of the world. The convention provides for proper management of fisheries in this region. Of particular importance is the fishery for jack mackerel off the coast of Chile, Peru, and Ecuador.

The South Pacific Fisheries Convention has already entered into force and now has 12 contracting parties. Ratification will enable the United States to take its seat at the table and have an equal voice in managing these fisheries.

As for the amendments to the Northwest Atlantic Convention, while the United States has already ratified the original convention in 1995 and has participated actively in the Northwest Atlantic Fisheries Organization, NAFO, ever since, the area covered by this agreement actually includes waters of the U.S. EEZ from Cape Hatteras to Maine. The original convention dates back to 1980 before the emergence of a number of key concepts in fisheries management. The amendments before the committee today essentially bring NAFO up to date. They will add rigor and transparency to NAFO's decisionmaking process, strengthen procedures for allocating catches, restraint overfishing, and adjust the formula for calculating dues.

The final agreement, on Port State Measures, is the first binding global agreement specifically intended to combat illegal, unreported, and unregulated, or IUU, fishing. The United States was among the first nations that signed the agreement when it was adopted in 2009. As we have already heard, IUU fishing undermines efforts to conserve and manage shared fish stocks and threatens the sustainability of all fisheries. Estimated global losses range from $10 to $23.5 billion each year.

Moreover, illegal fishing activities are often intertwined with drug trafficking, labor exploitation, environmental degradation, and organized crime. U.S. ratification will give us additional tools to address these problems.

Detecting IUU fishing at sea is difficult and expensive, but all fish caught at sea must ultimately come to port somewhere. The Port State Measures Agreement establishes standards for states to ensure that IUU-caught fish will not be landed, transshipped, packaged, or processed in their ports.

The United States took a leadership role in the development of this agreement. Timely ratification would again underscore the commitment of our Nation to strengthening efforts at the global and national level to deter, detect, and eliminate IUU fishing.

In closing, I would reiterate the importance of each of these agreements to the United States. Each one addresses a specific set of issues that, if not addressed, would threaten the sustainability of fisheries. Each has strong support from a broad and diverse range of U.S. stakeholders. We seek timely action by the Senate to provide its advice and consent to ratification.

Thank you very much. I would be pleased to answer any questions you may have.

[The prepared statement of Ambassador Balton follows:]

PREPARED STATEMENT OF AMBASSADOR DAVID A. BALTON

Mr. Chairman and members of the committee, I am Ambassador David Balton, Deputy Assistant Secretary of State for Oceans and Fisheries. I am pleased to testify before you today in support of the four international agreements being considered by the committee:

- The Convention on the Conservation and Management of High Seas Fisheries Resources of the North Pacific Ocean (hereinafter "NPFC Convention");
- The Convention on the Conservation and Management of High Seas Fishery Resources of the South Pacific Ocean (hereinafter "SPRFMO Convention");
- Amendments to the Convention on Future Multilateral Cooperation in the Northwest Atlantic Fisheries (hereinafter "NAFO Amendments"); and
- The FAO Agreement on Port State Measures to Prevent, Deter and Eliminate Illegal, Unreported and Unregulated Fishing (hereinafter the "Port State Measures Agreement" or "PSMA").

Individually and collectively, these four agreements represent significant progress in protecting U.S. interests, advancing our international policies and priorities to conserve and manage shared-living marine resources, to protect the broader marine environment from the effects of destructive fishing practices, and to prevent illegal fishing activities from undermining our global and regional efforts toward these ends. Each of these agreements has strong support from a broad range of stakeholders, including representatives of the U.S. fishing industry and the environmental and scientific communities, many of whom participated actively in the negotiations. For these reasons, we seek timely action by the Senate to provide its advice and consent to ratification.

The United States has a strong record of international leadership to conserve and manage shared fishery resources in a sustainable way. In fact, doing so is vitally important to our efforts to manage resources in waters under United States jurisdiction. The United States is already a party to more than a dozen such regional agreements governing such diverse resources as tunas in the Pacific and Atlantic Oceans, groundfish in the North Atlantic Ocean and the Bering Sea, salmon in the North Pacific and North Atlantic Oceans, among others. We are also a party to the two most significant fisheries agreements adopted at the global level—the 1993 FAO High Seas Fisheries Compliance Agreement and the 1995 U.N. Fish Stocks Agreement. Because activities that take place on the high seas and in waters under the jurisdiction of other countries can have a direct impact on important U.S. fisheries, being a member of these regimes—and especially having a seat at the table in these organizations—is imperative.

My colleague, Russell Smith, Deputy Assistant Secretary for International Fisheries at NOAA, will discuss the substance of these agreements from a conservation and management perspective and how their provisions support and enhance U.S. domestic fisheries management, while protecting the marine ecosystem. The remainder of my testimony will focus on how each of these agreements advances our international goals and objectives, including broad foreign policy objectives, and promotes responsible and sustainable use of our oceans resources.

NPFC CONVENTION

The NPFC Convention was adopted on February 24, 2012, signed by the United States on May 2, 2012, and transmitted to the Senate on April 22, 2013. Once in force, the Convention will establish the North Pacific Fisheries Commission (NPFC) through which the Parties will cooperate to ensure the long-term and sustainable use of fisheries in the Convention Area. U.S. accession to the Convention will protect and advance important and significant U.S. interests. In particular, the Convention Area includes areas of the high seas immediately adjacent to the U.S. exclusive economic zone (EEZ) off Alaska, the Pacific west coast, Hawaii, and other U.S. territories and possessions in the North Pacific. Thus, U.S. accession is vital to ensuring that the United States has a strong voice in managing fishing activities outside the U.S. EEZ that could have a direct impact on resources within waters under U.S. jurisdiction. U.S. accession will also ensure that U.S. fisherman will have a legitimate right to participate in fisheries within the Convention Area on an equitable basis.

As with the SPRFMO Convention, discussed below, negotiations toward the NPFC Convention were initiated in response to the growing concern of the international community toward the impacts of certain deep sea fishing practices, taking place outside areas of national jurisdiction, on a range of unique and endemic deep sea marine ecosystems including sea mounts, hydrothermal vents, deep sea and cold water coral communities, sponge fields, etc., collectively referred to as "vulnerable marine ecosystems."

This growing international concern was reflected most clearly in United Nations General Assembly (UNGA) Resolution 59/25, adopted on November 17, 2004, in which the UNGA: "[Called] upon States urgently to cooperate in the establishment of new regional fisheries management organizations or arrangements, where necessary and appropriate, with the competence to regulate bottom fisheries and the impacts of fishing on vulnerable marine ecosystems in areas where no such relevant organization or arrangement exists."

In response to this call, delegations from Japan, Korea, Russia, and the United States met in Tokyo, Japan, in August 2006, to begin negotiations that led to the 2012 adoption of the NPFC Convention. Initially, the negotiations had a much narrower focus than the Convention that is before you for consideration today. Between 2006 and 2008, the negotiations focused exclusively on bottom fisheries in the Northwest Pacific Ocean In particular, the discussions focused on bottom fisheries conducted by Japan, Korea, and Russia on the Emperor Seamounts, a chain of seamounts that extends from the North Hawaiian Ridge in the south, almost to the Aleutian Islands in the north.

As the discussions continued, the United States pressed, against some resistance, to expand the scope of the negotiations in two ways. First, our delegation pressed to expand the geographic scope of the Convention to ensure that the waters adjacent to the U.S. exclusive economic zone of Alaska and the Pacific west coast (Washington, Oregon, and California) were included within the Convention Area. Second, we pressed to ensure that the Convention established management authority not only for bottom fisheries, but for all high seas fishery resources not covered by an existing international management regime. Other than the bottom fisheries on the Emperor Seamounts, the primary pelagic fisheries included under this expanded scope include the fisheries for Pacific saury and squid. This expansion of the scope of the negotiations brought Canada, China, and Taiwan (which participated as the fishing entity of Chinese Taipei) into the negotiations, in addition to the original four States listed above.

The Convention will enter into force 180 days after receipt by the Depositary (the Government of Korea) of the fourth instrument of ratification, acceptance, approval, or accession. Japan was the first State to ratify the Convention. Canada, China, Korea, and Russia are all actively working to conclude their domestic procedures for ratification. As a result, there is a strong chance the Convention could enter into force in 2014 or early 2015.

Finally, Mr. Chairman, the United States has played an active and significant role in the development of the Convention and the preparations for its entry into force. At the request of the participating delegations, I was honored to chair the last several sessions of the negotiations that led to the adoption of the Convention in 2012. Since that time, one of my colleagues at the State Department has chaired the Preparatory Conference which has conducted the vital work to prepare for the entry into force of the Convention and the establishment of the new Commission. In order to continue to play such a leadership role, the United States must be at the table as a member of the Commission at its first meeting.

SPRFMO CONVENTION

The SPRFMO Convention was adopted on November 14, 2009, signed by the United States on January 31, 2011, and transmitted to the Senate on April 22, 2013. The Convention establishes the South Pacific Regional Fisheries Management Organization (SPRFMO) through which the Parties will cooperate to ensure the long-term and sustainable use of fisheries in the Convention Area. Although the United States currently has no fishing activity for fish stocks covered by the Convention, accession to the Convention will yield significant benefits to U.S. interests. The Convention Area includes areas of the high seas closest to the U.S. territory of American Samoa, and immediately adjacent to the U.S. exclusive economic zone off a number of U.S. Pacific possessions including Jarvis, Howland and Baker Islands, Kingman Reef and Palmyra Atoll. Here again, U.S. accession is vital to ensuring that the United States has a strong voice in managing fishing activities outside the U.S. EEZ that could have a direct impact on resources within waters under U.S. jurisdiction.

Moreover, to the extent that the NPFC and SPRFMO have comparable mandates for the North Pacific and South Pacific, respectively, the policies, practices, and agreements established under SPRFMO may well find resonance in the NPFC. As a result, active U.S. participation in SPRFMO will ensure that the work of SPRFMO results in such policies, practices, and agreements that would be acceptable to the United States in a broader context, including in the NPFC. Finally, as in the NPFC, U.S. accession to the SPRFMO Convention will ensure participatory rights for U.S. fishermen in fisheries within the Convention Area.

As with the NPFC Convention discussed above, negotiations for the SPRFMO Convention were initiated in response to the call by the UNGA for States to cooperate to establish new agreements related to bottom fishing and the impacts of fishing on vulnerable marine ecosystems in area where no such relevant organization or arrangement existed at the time.

Initial discussions on the establishment of such an organization took place between the Governments of Australia, Chile, and New Zealand in 2005. The discussions were quickly joined by a number of other countries and entities, including the United States, Belize, China, Denmark (in respect of the Faroe Islands), Ecuador, the European Union, Korea, Russia, Peru, several Pacific Island States, and Taiwan (again as the fishing entity of Chinese Taipei). As in the North Pacific negotiations, the scope of the negotiations expanded to include not only bottom fisheries but pelagic fish stocks not otherwise subject to management, the most significant of which is the fishery for jack mackerel off the coast of Chile, Peru, and Ecuador.

The SPRFMO Convention entered into force on August 24, 2012, and currently has 12 Contracting Parties. The Commission has met twice, in January 2013 and January 2014, and has adopted measures for the management of jack mackerel and bottom fishing. The United States has participated in the first two meetings of the Commission as an observer. As a result, our ability to influence any decisions taken is significantly less than would be the case if the United States were a full member of the Commission. Ratification of the Convention will allow the United States to take its seat at the table with the other members of the Commission and have an equal voice in matters before the Commission.

NAFO AMENDMENTS

The NAFO Amendments were adopted by the Northwest Atlantic Fisheries Organization (NAFO) September 28, 2007, and transmitted to the Senate on April 22, 2013. NAFO is charged with coordinating scientific study and cooperative management of the fisheries resources of the Northwest Atlantic Ocean, excluding salmon, tunas, and sedentary species of the Continental Shelf. The NAFO Convention Area includes the waters of the U.S. EEZ from Cape Hatteras to Maine, although NAFO management measures apply primarily in the high seas portion of the Convention Area.

The United States joined NAFO in 1995, and has participated actively since, assuming leadership positions and working to advance key principles of sustainable fisheries management. Although many NAFO stocks remain at levels too low to support fishing, others are finally showing signs of rebuilding under NAFO management. After working for many years to secure viable allocations, last year the United States was able to begin fisheries for some of these NAFO-managed high seas stocks.

Following international calls for regional fisheries management organizations to strengthen their effectiveness, NAFO launched a comprehensive reform process in 2005 intended to improve the way conservation and management measures are adopted, strengthen compliance and enforcement provisions, and revise its establishing Convention. The United States participated actively in this effort. Through it, we pushed to bring NAFO more in line with the principles of modern fisheries management and to address our particular concerns about catch allocations and fair participation.

The resulting comprehensive amendments met all of our priorities. They add additional rigor and transparency to the decisionmaking process, establish a dispute settlement procedure, improve the guiding language for allocating catches, formally incorporate key concepts including transparency and broader ecosystem considerations, and make the basis for calculating Contracting Parties' budget contributions more equitable.

The last point was a major U.S. priority. Under the Convention, part of the NAFO budget is divided equally among all Contracting Parties and the rest is split according to Parties' catches of certain species in the Convention Area, including within coastal States EEZs. As a result, coastal States such as the United States pay a disproportionately high share of NAFO's budget. The United States pushed to rebalance the dues to better match the benefits Parties receive. The amendments do not change the basic formula, but they amend the list of stocks used to calculate Parties' respective catches to include only species under NAFO management or for which NAFO provides scientific advice, and remove those fished exclusively in waters under a coastal State's jurisdiction. This change is expected to reduce U.S. dues by almost one-third.

The NAFO Amendments will take effect 120 days after Canada, as Depositary, receives notification of approval from nine Contracting Parties. To date five—Canada, Cuba, the European Union, Norway, and the Russian Federation—have deposited instruments of approval. We understand one other is imminent, and two others are expected by this fall. Speedy ratification may enable the United States to provide the last approval needed for the NAFO Amendments to take effect.

PORT STATE MEASURES AGREEMENT

The last Agreement I will discuss, Mr. Chairman, is different from the others. It is a global agreement, and is, in fact, the first binding global agreement specifically intended to combat illegal, unreported, and unregulated—or IUU—fishing. The United States signed the Port State Measures Agreement on November 22, 2009, and it was transmitted to the Senate November 14, 2011.

IUU fishing undermines efforts to conserve and manage shared fish stocks and threatens the sustainability of all fisheries. Estimates of global losses due to IUU fishing range from $10 to $23 billion each year. The large number of developing States that depend on fisheries for food security and export income are particularly vulnerable. A secondary benefit to ratification of the Port State Measures Agreement and the other treaties under consideration is that it will give the United States additional tools to address illegal activities that are often intertwined with IUU fishing, including drug trafficking, labor exploitation, environmental degradation, and organized crime.

Since IUU fishers can operate anywhere, detecting activities at sea is difficult and expensive. But, in order to sell or trade their illegal catch, they ultimately need to ensure that it is brought to a port for landing or transshipment. The Port State Measures Agreement establishes standards and requirements for port States to ensure IUU-caught fish will not be landed, transshipped, packaged, or processed in their ports.

Here again, the United States took a leadership role in the development of this agreement, hosting and Chairing the initial informal meetings that led to the agreement to engage in formal negotiations toward a legally binding instrument. Timely ratification would again underscore the commitment of the United States to strengthening efforts at the global and national levels to detect, deter, and eliminate IUU fishing.

CONCLUSION

In closing, I would simply reiterate the importance of each of these agreements to advancing U.S. economic interests and management objectives at the international level. Each of the agreements is crafted to address a specific set of issues that, if not addressed, threaten the sustainability of the fisheries resources in question. Each of them has strong support from a broad and diverse range of U.S. stakeholders from both the fishing industry and conservation community.

Senator RUBIO [presiding]. Thank you.

Before we move to Mr. Smith's testimony, just briefly to give you an insight to what is happening, there are all these important votes going on on the floor, so we are doing a relay race here. So Senator Markey has gone to cast his vote. When he returns, we will continue with the hearing. At some point it is possible we may have to have a short recess if we do not have enough members, because these are very important votes.

But, Mr. Smith, thank you for joining us.

STATEMENT OF RUSSELL F. SMITH III, DEPUTY ASSISTANT SECRETARY FOR INTERNATIONAL FISHERIES, NATIONAL OCEANIC AND ATMOSPHERIC ADMINISTRATION, U.S. DEPARTMENT OF COMMERCE, WASHINGTON, DC

Mr. SMITH. Thank you very much, Ranking Member Rubio, and I really appreciate the opportunity to testify here today on these important issues. I would ask that my testimony be included in the record of this hearing.

My name is Russell Smith and I am NOAA's Deputy Assistant Secretary for International Fisheries. Marine fish and fisheries, such as salmon in the Pacific Northwest, red snapper in the gulf, and cod in New England have long been vital to the economic strength and cultural identity of coastal communities in the United States. To ensure the long-term benefits of these resources, NOAA relies on clear, science-based rules, fair, effective, and consistent enforcement, and a shared commitment to sustainable management. The application of these standards has resulted in a Federal fishery management system that has made significant progress in ending overfishing and rebuilding our Nation's fisheries.

As a global leader in sustainably managing fisheries, the United States works to translate our domestic fishery management practices into international practices. The United States engages in international fisheries fora with the goal of ensuring that globally all fish stocks are sustainably managed.

One of the greatest challenges is combating illegal, unreported, and unregulated fishing. IUU is a global problem that threatens ocean ecosystems and the sustainable management of fisheries, as well as food security in coastal communities around the world. The economic losses resulting from IUU fishing are enormous. Experts estimate that they range from $10 to $23.5 billion per year.

U.S. accession to the four agreements that are the subject of today's hearing will directly benefit U.S. interests, fisheries-related and beyond. For example, the North Pacific and South Pacific and NAFO agreements manage fisheries in which U.S. vessels fish or areas adjacent to areas in which U.S. vessels fish. Some of the stocks managed under these agreements are also fished in U.S. waters.

Accession to these treaties will help level the playing field for U.S. fishers by allowing the United States to argue for foreign fishing fleets to be subject to the same high standards in international waters as our fleets adhere to in domestic waters. If our fleet ever wants the ability to fish in the areas managed by the new RFMOs, accession will put us in a better place to advocate for access to the international fishery.

The treaties also support the U.S. seafood industry and consumers by keeping illegal fisheries products out of U.S. and global markets, reducing competition with legal and sustainable American products.

These treaties will also support international sustainable fisheries management and thereby improve food security globally. As the United States imports more than 90 percent of its seafood, ensuring the sustainable management of global seafood fisheries stocks, including those in the North and South Pacific, helps to protect U.S. food security.

Let me briefly describe these treaties for you. The North Pacific and South Pacific Conventions establish commissions that are responsible for the long-term conservation and management of fisheries resources not covered under preexisting international agreements. They are also responsible for the protection of marine ecosystems in the convention area from fishing activities. Both agreements are based on modern principles of fisheries management establishing the use of a science-based and precautionary approach for developing conservation and management measures and a strong monitoring, control, and surveillance regime. In addition, the commission created under both agreements will establish mechanisms for monitoring compliance and responding to noncompliance.

NAFO is charged with coordinating scientific study and cooperative management of the fisheries resources of the Northwest Atlantic Ocean except for salmon, tuna, and sedentary species of the continental shelf. The updates to the NAFO convention put the organization in a better position to develop and implement measures based on sound advice, to use an ecosystem approach to fisheries management, and thereby to sustainably manage the stocks for which it is responsible. Additionally, the new convention strengthens NAFO's ability to combat IUU fishing.

Finally, the Port State Measures Agreement is the first binding global instrument focused specifically on combating IUU fishing. The agreement will help to keep IUU fish products from entering the stream of commerce by requiring port states to exercise better control over their ports. Port states will be required, with some limited exceptions, to keep IUU fishing vessels out of their ports and to deny them port services and to inspect a percentage of the fishing vessels that enter their ports.

With some of the largest and most successful fisheries in the world, the United States has become a global leader in the sustainable management of fisheries. These agreements allow us to advance those efforts.

Thank you again for the opportunity to testify before you today. I would be happy to take any questions that you may have.

[The prepared statement of Mr. Smith follows:]

PREPARED STATEMENT OF RUSSELL F. SMITH III

INTRODUCTION

Good morning Mr. Chairman and members of the committee. I am Russell Smith, Deputy Assistant Secretary for International Fisheries, National Oceanic and Atmospheric Administration (NOAA), Department of Commerce. Thank you very much for the opportunity to come before you today to discuss four international fisheries agreements intended to improve the conservation and management of specific international fisheries and to combat illegal, unreported, and unregulated (IUU) fishing.

Before I address the four treaties, I wish to provide some context about why they are important to U.S. national interest. Marine fish and fisheries, such as salmon in the Pacific Northwest and cod in New England, have been vital to the prosperity and cultural identity of coastal communities in the United States. U.S. fisheries play an enormous role in the U.S. economy. Commercial fishing supports fishers and fishing communities, and provides Americans with a sustainable, healthy food source. The seafood industry in the U.S.—harvesters, seafood processors and dealers, seafood wholesalers and seafood retailers, including imports and multiplier effects—generated $129 billion in sales impacts and $37 billion in income impacts, and supported 1.2 million jobs in 2011.[1] Recreational fishing also makes significant contributions to employment and the economy in the United States. Recreational fishing generated an estimated $56 billion in sales impacts, $18 billion in income impacts, and supported 364,000 jobs in 2011.[2] Subsistence fishing provides an essential food source and is culturally significant for indigenous peoples.

To ensure the long-term benefits of these resources to the American people, NOAA relies on clear, science-based rules, fair, effective and consistent enforcement, and a shared commitment to sustainable management. Much of this work occurs under the Magnuson-Stevens Fishery Conservation and Management Act (Magnuson-Stevens Act), which sets forth standards for the conservation, management, and sustainable use of our Nation's fisheries resources. The application of these standards has resulted in a federal fishery management system that has made very significant progress in ending overfishing and rebuilding our Nation's fisheries.

The United States is also one of the world's largest importers and consumers of seafood. In 2011, seafood imports contributed 176,000 jobs, $48.4 billion in sales impacts, and $14.8 billion in value added impacts.[3] As such, the United States is in a unique position to support sustainable fisheries around the world while providing a level playing field for our domestic fishermen. Working in collaboration with the Department of State and the U.S. Coast Guard, NOAA engages in international fisheries fora, such as Regional Fisheries Management Organizations (RFMOs), to ensure that global fish stocks are sustainably managed, including by ensuring that management is based on the best available science. As the United States is a leader in sustainably managing fisheries, often we seek to draw from our experience and convince RFMOs to apply, in the waters under their jurisdiction, management measures comparable to those applied in U.S. waters.

One of the greatest challenges to our international efforts to ensure the sustainable management of global fisheries is combating illegal, unreported, or unregulated (IUU) fishing. IUU fishing is a global problem that threatens ocean ecosystems and impacts fisheries, food security, and coastal communities around the world. Experts estimate the global value of economic losses from IUU fishing range between $10 and $23.5 billion.[4] By circumventing conservation and management measures, companies and individuals engaging in IUU fishing cut corners and lower their operating costs. As a result, their illegally caught products provide unfair competition for law-abiding fishermen and seafood industries in the marketplace, and can undercut the sustainability of international and U.S. fisheries.[5]

U.S. accession to the four agreements before you today would greatly strengthen our ability to sustainably manage fisheries resources globally and combat IUU fishing. The agreements are: the Convention on the Conservation and Management of High Seas Fisheries Resources in the North Pacific Ocean (or North Pacific Convention); the Convention on the Conservation and Management of High Seas Fishery Resources in the South Pacific Ocean (or South Pacific Convention); the Amendment to the Convention on Future Multilateral Cooperation in the Northwest Atlantic Fisheries (or NAFO Convention Amendment); and the Agreement on Port State Measures to Prevent, Deter and Eliminate Illegal, Unreported and Unregulated Fishing (or Port States Agreement).

These four treaties will directly benefit U.S. interests. The new RFMOs in the North and South Pacific and the existing RFMO in the Northwest Atlantic (NAFO) will have management authority for target stocks and bycatch species that straddle U.S. waters. By joining these organizations and strengthening their management regimes, the United States can promote the use of our strong fishery management principles internationally so that foreign fishing fleets abide by the same standards as our industry. In joining the new North and South Pacific RFMOs, we are also ensuring future economic opportunities for our domestic fishing interests. Although there is currently no U.S. industry operating within the North or South Pacific RFMOs, our membership will allow for the possibility of future engagement and provide the opportunity for the U.S. to influence the management and compliance monitoring measures adopted by these organizations.

The treaties also support the U.S. seafood industry and consumers by keeping illegal fisheries product out of U.S. and global markets. The North and South Pacific RFMOs and NAFO will implement new and strengthen existing management tools to combat IUU fishing within their areas. Moreover, the Port States Agreement will help to keep IUU fishing products from entering the market, and keep them from competing with U.S. caught, sustainably harvested, legal seafood. Denying port entry and access to port services, and consequently preventing illegal seafood from entering trade, increases the costs associated with IUU fishing operations and removes the financial incentives for engaging in IUU fishing.

Lastly, these treaties will support international sustainable fisheries management and thereby improve food security globally. Seafood is a significant source of protein for nearly 3 billion people and is the planet's most highly traded food commodity, contributing to the livelihoods of more than 560 million people.[6] IUU fishing threatens food security and socioeconomic stability in many parts of the world by reducing the productivity and profitability of legitimate fisheries, including artisanal fisheries in coastal areas. By improving the management of fisheries through these new or updated RFMOs, coupled with the IUU fishing-combating Port States Agreement, the four treaties address food security in developing coastal states, in the United States and globally; and thereby support the political stability of U.S. interests worldwide.

I now will describe each of the four agreements and the benefits they would provide in more detail.

NORTH PACIFIC AND SOUTH PACIFIC FISHERIES CONVENTIONS

The United States has worked for many years with other nations to improve the management of fisheries at the international level and to protect vulnerable marine ecosystems from the impacts of certain fishing practices on the high seas. The North Pacific and South Pacific Conventions will advance U.S. interests in the effective management of high seas fisheries. U.S. participation in the Commissions established under the North Pacific and South Pacific Conventions will facilitate development of measures adopted for fisheries on the high seas of the Pacific Ocean that are compatible with measures adopted by the United States with respect to fisheries in adjacent waters under the fisheries jurisdiction of the United States. In addition, U.S. participation will ensure that future U.S. fishing interests subject to the North Pacific and South Pacific Conventions can be factored into allocation decisions. Furthermore, as both the South Pacific Convention area and the North Pacific Convention areas overlap with that of other Pacific RFMOs in which the United States is a party, U.S. participation will help to ensure a consistent approach to conservation and management among these RFMOs and across the Pacific.

North Pacific Convention

The North Pacific Convention establishes a new regional fisheries management organization, the North Pacific Fisheries Commission (NPFC), through which Parties will cooperate to ensure the long-term conservation and sustainable use of fisheries resources in the Convention Area while protecting the marine ecosystems of the North Pacific Ocean in which these resources occur. The North Pacific Convention Area is the high seas area (i.e., outside of 200-mile EEZs) roughly north of 20-degrees North latitude and south of the Aleutians. The specific geographic coordinates of the North Pacific Convention Area are delineated in Article 4 of the Convention. Cooperation under the North Pacific Convention will address fisheries resources not covered under preexisting international fisheries management instruments and will help to prevent significant adverse impacts on vulnerable marine ecosystems on the high seas that may have impacts on fisheries resources in areas subject to U.S. jurisdiction. One of the general principles of the North Pacific Convention is that conservation and management measures established for straddling fish stocks on the high seas and those adopted for areas under national jurisdiction should be compatible to ensure conservation and management of these fisheries resources in their entirety.

The North Pacific Convention calls for a science-based and precautionary approach to the management of fisheries resources and a strong monitoring, control, and surveillance regime. It also will establish two committees, a Scientific Committee and a Technical and Compliance Committee, to carry out its functions. The North Pacific Convention will also allow for the meaningful participation of Taiwan as a fishing entity in the NPFC.

Of particular concern to the NPFC are bottom fisheries over seamounts that could have significant adverse impacts on vulnerable marine ecosystems. The participants to the negotiations of the North Pacific Convention have already agreed to interim measures to protect vulnerable marine ecosystems and the sustainable management of high seas bottom fisheries in the North Pacific Convention Area. The interim measures include requiring assessments prior to any fishing that demonstrate that contemplated fishing activities would not have significant adverse impacts on vulnerable marine ecosystems and sustainability of the fishery resources.

While there are presently no U.S. vessels fishing whose activities would be covered by the North Pacific Convention, there have been in the past and may be in the future. The United States is a coastal State with fisheries and marine habitats adjacent to the North Pacific Convention Area. Those fisheries can be impacted by management measures adopted by the North Pacific Commission.

For example, since 1986, NMFS has prohibited fishing in the U.S. EEZ for Pacific armorhead, one of the groundfish species that will be managed in the Convention area. Armorhead are overfished as a result of past over-exploitation by foreign vessels in international waters dating back to the 1970s or earlier. NMFS believes that continued exploitation outside our EEZ by foreign fleets has kept the stock in an overfished condition. The Hancock Seamounts are the only known armorhead habitat within our EEZ. These seamounts lie west of 180° W. and north of 28° N., to the northwest of Kure Atoll in the Northwestern Hawaiian Islands. The Western Pacific Fishery Management Council and NMFS have responded to the overfished condition of armorhead by implementing a moratorium on catching armorhead and related seamount groundfish. The Council and NMFS recognize that, because less than 5 percent of the armorhead habitat lies within U.S. jurisdiction, rebuilding of the stock must be accomplished through coordinated international management. The North Pacific Convention is an important vehicle to achieve such coordinated international management.

The United States also has fleets operating in the North Pacific Convention Area that are fishing for tunas, swordfish, and other species that are subject to the jurisdiction of other RFMOs which could cooperate with the NPFC.

South Pacific Convention

The South Pacific Convention establishes a new regional fisheries management organization, the South Pacific Regional Fisheries Management Organization (SPRFMO) through which Parties will cooperate in the conservation and sustainable use of the high seas fishery resources in the South Pacific Ocean and safeguard the marine ecosystems in which these resources occur.

The South Pacific Convention applies to areas of the South Pacific outside national jurisdiction from Australia to South America. Some of these areas abut the U.S. EEZ. The initial objectives of the negotiators were to develop a management framework to control bottom fishing in the western Pacific, primarily by New Zealand, Australia, and Taiwan, and the jack mackerel fishery in the eastern Pacific, primarily by Chile, Peru, and the European Union. The United States was a primary participant in the negotiation of the South Pacific Convention. SPRFMO will address fisheries resources not currently under management by preexisting agreements, such as new pelagic fisheries or expanded fisheries for stocks that straddle one or more exclusive economic zones and high seas areas beyond them.

The South Pacific Convention requires Parties to apply specific conservation and management principles and approaches in giving effect to the objective of the South Pacific Convention. These principles and approaches are enshrined in existing international instruments to which the United States is a party, such as the 1995 Fish Stocks Agreement. These standards highlight the importance of using the best-available science and applying an ecosystem approach to fisheries management. In addition, the South Pacific Convention requires that Parties design and adopt specific conservation and management measures such as limitations on catch or effort, time or area closures, and gear restrictions.

While there are presently no U.S. vessels fishing in the high seas areas of the South Pacific whose activities would be covered by the South Pacific Convention, U.S. membership within the Commission would allow for the potential participation of future fishing interests and enable the U.S. to influence the development of new and amended conservation and management measures.

NAFO Convention Amendment

The Northwest Atlantic Fisheries Organization (NAFO) is charged with coordinating scientific study and cooperative management of the fisheries resources of the Northwest Atlantic Ocean, excluding salmon, tuna, and sedentary species of the Continental Shelf. It was established in 1979 by the Convention on Future Multilateral Cooperation in the Northwest Atlantic Fisheries (the ''Convention''). The United States acceded to the Convention in 1995 and has participated actively in NAFO since that time, often assuming leadership positions and working to advance key principles of sustainable fisheries management.

In 2005, NAFO launched a reform effort designed to streamline the Organization and bring it more in line with the principles of modern fisheries management. In 2007, NAFO members adopted the NAFO Convention Amendment, which is comprehensive, touching on every element of the Convention. It addresses specific U.S. concerns and incorporates key international fisheries governance approaches, as found in the 1995 Fish Stocks Agreement, the 1993 Food and Agriculture Organization of the United Nations (FAO) Compliance Agreement, and more recent regional fisheries management agreements. The NAFO Convention Amendment vastly improves the ability of NAFO and its membership to effectively manage the resources under its purview and the ecosystems associated with those resources.

Key elements of the NAFO Convention Amendment include provisions that detail NAFO's objectives, including long-term conservation and sustainable use of fishery resources and safeguarding of marine ecosystems in the convention area. The agreement also outlines general principles that include (among many others) promoting optimum use and long-term sustainability of fishery resources, adopting management measures based on the best scientific advice available, applying the precautionary approach when there is scientific uncertainty, taking into account the effect of fishing on the marine ecosystem, and highlighting the need to preserve biodiversity. This language reflects a modernized approach to fisheries management.

Furthermore, the amendment simplifies the structure of NAFO, which will now consist of a Commission, a Scientific Council, and a Secretariat. This new structure combines the current General Council and Fisheries Commission into a single Commission and reorganizes a number of the subbodies. These changes will streamline NAFO considerably and result in increased efficiency, more effective conservation and management, and reduced costs. The NAFO Convention Amendment enables the Commission to take action, including nondiscriminatory trade-related measures, against any State or fishing entity whose fishing vessels undermine the effectiveness of NAFO measures. It also requires the Scientific Council to advise the Commission on the impacts of fishing on the marine ecosystem as a whole within the Convention Area. Finally, the amendment describes the formulation of the Organization's budget and the calculation of the contributions due by each Contracting Party. One important result of changes to the amendment is that U.S. costs associated with membership in NAFO will be considerably reduced.

The NAFO Convention Amendment also describes Contracting Party duties, flag State duties, and port State duties, respectively. These provisions are noteworthy because they draw on international fisheries governance approaches found in the most important and innovative international agreements on fisheries management including the 1995 Fish Stocks Agreement, the 1993 FAO Compliance Agreement, and more recent regional fisheries management agreements. The language primarily focuses on effective implementation of measures adopted by NAFO, reporting requirements, inspections, and compliance and enforcement obligations.

The NAFO Convention Amendment rewrites the old provisions for decision-making, implementation, and settlement of disputes. It modifies the current general rule for decisionmaking within the Commission from a simple majority to consensus and outlines voting rules to be applied, namely a two-thirds majority, if consensus is not possible. The process for implementation of Commission decisions is also substantially modified, and the NAFO Convention Amendment details how and when decisions become binding and introduces changes to the existing objection procedure. The revised objection procedure is an improvement as it, among other things, requires a detailed explanation from the objecting Contracting Party and a declaration of the actions (including alternative measures) to be taken. Objecting Parties or the Commission may also now submit matters to an ad hoc panel and/or invoke the new dispute settlement procedures, which provide the choice of a number of fora in which to seek resolutions through peaceful means. The process also requires Contracting Parties to submit disputes to compulsory proceedings pursuant to the 1995 Fish Stocks Agreement.

The NAFO Convention Amendment addresses cooperation with non-Contracting Parties and with other organizations. These new provisions are designed to ensure that non-Contracting flag State vessels abide by NAFO measures when fishing in the NAFO Regulatory Area. They call for exchange of information on fishing activities of non-Contracting Parties and measures to deter activities (such as IUU fishing) that may undermine the measures adopted by the Commission. The new text further calls on NAFO to cooperate with the FAO and other relevant organizations, including RFMOs. This is particularly important with respect to the success of regional and global efforts relating to IUU fishing, trade tracking, and even for implementing the ecosystem management of fisheries.

Other amendment provisions are administrative in nature (e.g., establishing procedures for review and amendment of the Convention and its Annexes). Annex I to the Convention, "Scientific and Statistical Subareas, Divisions and Subdivisions," provides the coordinates of the scientific and statistical subareas, divisions and subdivisions of the Convention Area. Annex II to the Convention, "Rules Concerning the Ad Hoc Panel Procedure pursuant to Article XV," is a new Annex describing the procedure for the ad hoc panels, one method available to settle disputes between Contracting Parties.

Port States Agreement

The Agreement on Port State Measures to Prevent, Deter, and Eliminate Illegal, Unreported and Unregulated Fishing is the first binding global instrument focused specifically to combat IUU fishing. It recognizes that all fish must pass through a port to get to market and that port States can take cost-effective measures to combat IUU fishing. IUU fishing deprives law-abiding fishermen and coastal communities around the world of up to an estimated $23.5 billion of seafood and seafood products every year,[7] and undermines efforts to monitor and sustainably manage fisheries. It also threatens the food security in some of the poorest countries in the world as well as in the United States and interferes with the livelihood of legitimate fishers around the world. Seafood caught through IUU fishing enters the global marketplace through ports all around the world. Preventing that fish from entering the global market requires an international solution and the cooperation of countries throughout the world.

The Port States Agreement is recognized within the international community as a landmark in the effort to combat IUU fishing. The United States was a primary participant in its negotiation and was one of the first countries to sign it. We took a leadership role because we recognized how important taking these measures is for nations that want to ensure that product entering their ports has been legally harvested and is safe for consumers. We have had experience with the implementation of most of the substantive measures in the agreement as most of these measures are already contained in U.S. law.

The agreement has already had significant impact on efforts to combat IUU fishing, influencing the adoption of similar measures by various RFMOs and providing a model for nations, developing nations in particular, to follow in establishing or strengthening dockside inspection programs. However, the full effect of the Port States Agreement as a tool to combat IUU fishing will not be realized until its entry into force, which requires ratification by 25 nations or regional economic integration organizations. So far, nine have done so. Ratification of the Port States Agreement by the United States will demonstrate strong leadership in the global battle against IUU fishing and will position the United States to encourage ratification by other countries.

The agreement sets forth minimum standards for the conduct of dockside inspections and training of inspectors and, most significantly, requires parties to restrict port entry and port services for foreign vessels known or suspected of having been involved in IUU fishing, particularly those on a RFMO IUU fishing vessel list. These minimum standards would increase the risks and costs associated with IUU fishing activities and help to ensure that IUU fish and fish products do not enter into global trade. Senate advice and consent to ratification of the Port States Agreement will ultimately benefit U.S. fishermen, seafood buyers, and consumers by preventing IUU vessels from entering our ports and diluting the market with illegal product.

The Port States Agreement has four primary sets of obligations that Parties are required to apply vis-a-vis foreign flagged fishing vessels (including support vessels) seeking entry to a Party's port:

- Parties are required to designate ports to which foreign-flagged vessels may seek entry, to require that certain information be collected and considered, and to establish a process for granting or denying port entry and/or the use of port services to foreign-flagged fishing vessels;
- Parties must maintain the capacity to conduct dockside vessel inspections in the designated ports and adhere to minimum standards for the conduct of inspections and the training of inspectors. A sufficient number of inspections must be conducted to satisfy the objective of the agreement;
- Subject to certain limited exceptions, Parties must deny port entry and the use of port services to vessels that have been engaged in IUU fishing, including as indicated by inclusion of the vessel on an RFMO IUU Vessel list. Importantly, the limited exceptions include allowing port entry exclusively for enforcement purposes or in the event of force majeure; and,
- Parties are required to share information, including inspection results, with the flag States and, as appropriate, other relevant Parties and entities, as well as to take followup actions as requested by the flag State when evidence of IUU fishing is found during the course of an inspection.

NOAA would be the lead agency for U.S. implementation of the Port States Agreement. Primary responsibility to carry out its obligations, particularly those related to vessel inspections, will fall on NOAA's National Marine Fisheries Service (NMFS), Office of Law Enforcement, in collaboration with the U.S. Coast Guard, which has Captain of the Port authority for the United States. Importantly, the minimum standards set by the Port States Agreement track closely to what the United States already does. Under the Port States Agreement, these best practices would become common practice around the world, thereby effectively closing the so-called ports of convenience that IUU fishing operators use to land their fish and support their activities. As a global leader in sustainable fishing practices, and the third-largest importer of seafood in the world, the United States has a responsibility to ensure the fish we import is caught legally. The United States also has a responsibility to protect our domestic fishermen from unfair competition and ensure consumer confidence in the seafood supply by keeping illegal product out of the market. The Port State Measures Agreement marks a significant step forward on both of these counts.

The United States, with our strong legal frameworks, experience in effective port management and robust fisheries law enforcement, has been assisting developing nations in their preparations for implementation of the agreement. NOAA has most recently assisted Indonesia in its development of training curriculum for fisheries inspectors who will carry out inspections under the agreement. Additionally, the United States has strongly promoted the adoption of measures in RFMOs that strengthen port related measures, in accordance with the agreement. These efforts promote the success of the agreement and thereby reduce the amount of IUU product entering our domestic markets.

CONCLUSION

Mr. Chairman and Members of the Committee, the Department of State, the Department of Commerce, the U.S. Coast Guard, and U.S. stakeholders strongly support these four international fisheries agreements. All of these agreements will contribute to the sustainable management of internationally shared fisheries resources and directly impact U.S. interests. The four agreements promote U.S. interests by (1) leveling the playing field for U.S. fishing industry by bringing foreign fishers up to the standards applied to U.S. fishers, (2) keeping illegal product from entering the U.S. and global markets and thereby supporting legal, sustainably harvested U.S. seafood products, and (3) promoting sustainable fisheries internationally which supports food security and political stability globally. U.S. accession will allow us to be at the table to further those interests.

End Notes

[1] See Fisheries Economics of the U.S. 2011. NMFS Office of Science & Technology, available at:http://www.st.nmfs.noaa.gov/economics/publications/feus/fisheries1economics12011.

[2] Sabrina J. Lovell, Scott Steinback, and James Hilger. 2013. The Economic Contribution of Marine Angler Expenditures in the United States, 2011. U.S. Dep. Commerce, NOAA Tech. Memo. NMFS–F/SPO–134, 188 p.

[3] See Fisheries Economics of the U.S. 2011, at 7.

[4] Agnew DJ, J. Pearce, G. Pramod, T. Peatman, R. Watson, et al. (2009). Estimating the worldwide extent of illegal fishing. PLoS ONE, 4(2): e4570.

[5] United Nations Office of Drugs and Crime. "Issue Paper—Transnational Organized Crime in the Fishing Industry" http://www.unodc.org/documents/human-trafficking/Issue1Paper1-1TOC1in1the1Fishing1Industry.pdf.   2011.

[6] United Nations Interagency Framework Team for Preventive Action. "Renewable Resources and   Conflict."   http://www.un.org/en/events/environmentconflictday/pdf/GN1Renewable1 Consultation.pdf. 2012.

[7] Agnew DJ, J. Pearce, G. Pramod, T. Peatman, R. Watson, et al. (2009). Estimating the worldwide extent of illegal fishing. PLoS ONE, 4(2): e4570.

Senator RUBIO. Thank you, Mr. Smith. I would just note, without objection, that your full comments will be included in the committee's record.

Admiral, I hate to do this to you. We are going to have to take a brief, 10-minute recess while I go vote, because the majority leader is pushing these through pretty quickly. I anticipate that the chairman will be back here in a moment so we can continue. So if you would just give us about 10 minutes, I think, and we will be back.

The committee stands in recess for 10 minutes.

[Recess from 3:05 p.m. to 3:10 p.m.]

Senator MARKEY [presiding]. The committee will come to order, and we are now joined by Senator Murkowski, who is the cochair of the Oceans Caucus. Her cochair, Sheldon Whitehouse, has already testified. We welcome you, Senator.

Whenever you are comfortable, please begin.

STATEMENT OF HON. LISA MURKOWSKI, U.S. SENATOR FROM ALASKA

Senator MURKOWSKI. Thank you, Mr. Chairman, Ranking Member Rubio, and to other members of the committee who are not here today, but who hopefully have an opportunity to view the testimony, thank you for the opportunity to speak today on some very important treaties facing the U.S. Senate and before your committee here at Foreign Relations.

Taking the time to address these fisheries treaties is critically important, particularly the effects of IUU fishing and activities on U.S. interests. Senator Whitehouse and I have been working as co-chairs of the Senate Oceans Caucus to be strong advocates for our Nation's oceans and fisheries. I think it is critically important that as we look to protect the strength of our fisheries, the strength of our oceans, that we understand that our oceans know no boundaries, in the sense that we know where the borders are of our States, we know where the borders are of our countries, but we need to ensure that as we are working with other nations as it relates to our fisheries that we have some common framework.

I am here today because the fishing and the seafood industries are vital economic drivers in my State. Alaska's fisheries are the most abundant and sustainably managed in the Nation and we are quite proud of that. We lead all States in terms of both volume and value of commercial fisheries, with approximately 1.84 million metric tons, worth $1.3 billion. We account for over 52 percent of the Nation's commercial seafood harvest. Alaska's commercial, sport, and subsistence fisheries are at the heart of coastal Alaska. They are the economic livelihood for more than 80,000 Alaskans who are either directly or indirectly employed in the industry.

The witnesses that you have today will give great overview of these important issues. They can address the international and the domestic implications of the treaties that you have before you. You do have an individual on the third panel, Mark Gleason, who is with the Alaska Bering Sea Crabbers. I appreciate the fact that he has traveled to D.C. today to testify on behalf of the organization.

You might not have heard of the Bering Sea Crabbers, but most people are at least familiar with ''The Deadliest Catch.'' All you need to do is think of ''Deadliest Catch'' and it takes you into the activities of the Bering Sea.

Some of you may not know that I have a little bit of an interest in not only the crab fishery, but safety at sea. My son just finished up a season in the Bering Sea crabbing. They left last night through Unimak Pass to travel across the Gulf of Alaska. He is headed back home and he is probably going to have some Bering Sea crab stories that I am not sure that his mother is really ready to hear yet, but I am bracing myself.

But as I think about the experience that my son has had as a Bering Sea crab fishermen, given what we have put in place with safeties and precautions and protocols, it is a much better world now for our crabbers and our fishermen than it was just a few years ago.

It is important, however, that Alaska and U.S. fishermen have a level playing field when it comes to our harvesting opportunities. Russian IUU crab has been a serious problem for Alaska since at least 1990. As is true for most commodity markets, crab prices of course are driven by supply. IUU crab lowers the market price to fishermen and processors and tax revenues to our State.

The estimated impacts of IUU crab to harvesters since the year 2000 is about $560 million, with an additional cost to crab processing ports of over a million dollars in lost landing revenues. These are real dollars that we are talking about. This is real impact to a State.

As recently as 2011, NOAA law enforcement seized 112 metric tons of illegally harvested Russian king crab that was being shipped to United States markets through the port of Seattle. So I am pleased to be followed by representatives from the Coast Guard, NOAA, and the State Department who will speak in more detail on their efforts to prevent IUU seafood from entering the United States. These three agencies, with assistance from the U.S. Customs and Border Patrol, and the FDA, successfully prosecuted the case and helped shut down one avenue for illegal imports. I think this is a positive example and I believe the treaties before you will enhance the effectiveness of U.S. authority to deter IUU activities.

Two of the treaties that you have, the Port State Measures Agreement and the Convention on the Conservation and Management of High Seas Fisheries Resources in the North Pacific, are very important to my State's fishermen. The first sets global standards to combat IUU fishing. It will help to protect U.S. fishermen by keeping foreign illegally caught fish from entering the global stream of commerce. Specifically, it establishes global port restrictions designed to catch vessels engaged in illegal fishing activities when they attempt to offload the fish in port.

The second will establish a new regional fishery management organization for fisheries resources located near the North Pacific and not currently addressed through preexisting international fisheries management bodies.

I would like to comment, Mr. Chairman, on the fact that IUU vessels can also be some pretty bad actors beyond the world of fishing. You are going to be hearing testimony from the third panel on the role that IUU vessels are playing in the context of human trafficking and drug smuggling. While these particular fishing treaties are not focused on these issues specifically, it is my understanding that they will provide additional tools that can help U.S. law enforcement officials crack down on them as well.

Again, I truly appreciate, and I know that my colleague Senator Whitehouse does as well, the efforts of this committee to look into these issues, to discuss them thoroughly, to advance these treaties through the Senate, and help to level the playing field for U.S. fisheries.

With that, Mr. Chairman, I am happy to take any questions that you might briefly have. I appreciate the allowance and indulgence of your time in allowing me to pop in as we juggle votes. Thank you.

[The prepared statement of Senator Murkowski follows:]

PREPARED STATEMENT OF SENATOR LISA MURKOWSKI

Mr. Chairman, Ranking Member Rubio, other members of the committee who were not able to make it here today, but who hopefully will have an opportunity to review this testimony, thank you for this opportunity to speak today on some very important treaties in front of the U.S. Senate and before the Foreign Relations Committee. Taking the time to address these fisheries treaties is critically important, particularly with regard to the effects of IUU fishing activities on U.S. interests. Senator Whitehouse and I have been working as cochairs of the Senate Oceans Caucus to be strong advocates for our Nation's oceans and fisheries. I think it is critically important that as we look to protect the strength of our fisheries, the strength of our oceans, that we understand that our oceans know no boundaries. I mean this in the sense that we know where the borders are for our states, where the borders are for countries, but we need to ensure that as we work with other nations to protect our fisheries outside our national jurisdiction, that we work within the common framework of international agreements.

I am here because the fishing and seafood industries are vital economic drivers in my home State. Alaska's fisheries are the most abundant and sustainably managed in the Nation, and we are quite proud of that fact. Alaska leads all States in terms of both volume and value of commercial fisheries with approximately 1.84 million metric tons worth $1.3 billion—accounting for over 52 percent of the Nation's commercial seafood harvests. Alaska's commercial, sport, and subsistence fisheries are at the heart of coastal Alaska and they are the source of economic livelihood for more than 80,000 Alaskans who are directly or indirectly employed in the industry.

The witnesses you have assembled for today's hearing will provide an excellent overview of this important issue, and can address the international and domestic implications of the treaties before you. You do have an individual on the third panel, Mark Gleason, who is with the Alaska Bering Sea Crabbers, and I appreciate the fact that he has traveled to D.C. to testify on behalf of his organization. Now you may not have heard of the Alaska Bering Sea Crabbers, but most people are at least familiar with the Deadliest Catch. All you need to do is think of Deadliest Catch and it takes you into the activities out in the Bering Sea. Some of you may not know that I have a little bit of an interest not only in the crab fishery, but in the safety of fishing vessels out in the Bering Sea. My son just finished up a season crabbing in the Bering Sea, and they left last night through Unimak Pass to travel across the Gulf of Alaska. He is headed back home and he probably is going to have some Bering Sea crab stories that I am not sure his mother is really ready to hear yet, but I am bracing myself. As I think about the experience my son has had as a Bering Sea crab fisherman, given what we in the U.S. have put in place for safety, it is a much better situation out there for our crabbers and our fishermen. The same is true in terms of the fisheries management regimes we have in place in the U.S., and it is important that Alaskan and U.S. fishermen have a level playing field as they compete in the global seafood market.

Russian IUU crab has been a serious problem for Alaska since at least 1990. As is true for most commodity markets, crab prices are driven by supply. IUU crab lowers the market price to fishermen and processors, and tax revenues to the State of Alaska. The estimated impacts of IUU crab to harvesters since 2000 is about $560 million, with an additional cost to crab processing ports of over $11 million in lost landing tax revenues. These are real dollars we are talking about, this has a real impact on my State.

As recently as 2011, NOAA law enforcement seized 112 metric tons of illegally harvested Russian king crab that was being shipped to U.S. markets through the Port of Seattle. I am pleased to be followed by representatives from the U.S. Coast Guard, NOAA, and the State Department who will speak in more detail on their efforts to prevent IUU seafood from entering the U.S. These three agencies, with assistance from U.S Customs and Border Patrol and the FDA, successfully prosecuted this case and helped shut down one avenue for illegal imports. This is one positive example, and I believe the treaties before you will enhance the effectiveness of U.S. authority to deter IUU activities.

Two of the treaties you have before you today, the Port State Measures Agreement and the Convention on the Conservation and Management of High Seas Fisheries Resources in the North Pacific Ocean, are of particular interest to my State's fishermen. The first will set global standards to combat IUU fishing. We have high standards in the U.S., and this treaty will help to protect U.S. fishermen by keeping foreign illegally caught fish from entering the global stream of commerce. Specifically, it will establish global port restrictions designed to catch vessels engaged in illegal fishing activities when they attempt to offload fish in port.

The second will establish a new Regional Fishery Management Organization (RFMO), the North Pacific Fisheries Commission, for fisheries resources located near the North Pacific Ocean, and not currently addressed through preexisting international fisheries management bodies. This region is adjacent to Alaska, and the west coast, and it is important to ensure that there is a fisheries management regime in place to deter IUU fishing activities.

Before concluding, I would like to comment on the fact that IUU vessels also can be pretty bad actors beyond the world of fishing. You will be hearing testimony from the third panel on the role that IUU vessels are playing in the context of human trafficking and drug smuggling. While these fisheries treaties are not focused on these issues specifically, it is my understanding that they will provide additional tools that can help U.S. law enforcement officials crack down on them as well.

Again, I truly appreciate, and I know that my colleague, Senator Whitehouse, does as well, the efforts of this committee to look into these issues, to discuss them thoroughly, and to advance these treaties to level the playing field for U.S. fishermen.

I encourage the committee to consider these treaties favorably, and to move them forward for consideration by the full Senate.

Senator MARKEY. We appreciate your leadership, Senator Murkowski, on this set of critical issues, and we intend on acting, and your leadership has played a big role in bringing us to this space. So we thank you so much for your service.

We would ask the second panel to come back up and we will move to Admiral Kenney, although your nameplate says "Kennedy." In Massachusetts that is not a bad thing, not a bad thing. Most people would not change their name from Kennedy to Kenney in Massachusetts, the way we just did for you.

STATEMENT OF REAR ADMIRAL FREDERICK J. KENNEY, JUDGE ADVOCATE GENERAL AND CHIEF COUNSEL, U.S. COAST GUARD, WASHINGTON, DC

Admiral KENNEY. Well, thank you, Senator. I am from Massachusetts and——

Senator MARKEY. Really? What high school?

Admiral KENNEY [continuing]. What is that?

Senator MARKEY. What high school?

Admiral KENNEY. I went to Rossview Latin School.

Senator MARKEY. Really? A very well educated witness before us. [Laughter.]

So whenever you are ready, Admiral, please begin.

Admiral KENNEY. But it is an honor to be confused with that other illustrious Massachusetts family.

Well, good afternoon, Chairman Markey. It is a pleasure to appear before you to discuss how the international fisheries treaties before you today will improve the Coast Guard's ability to deter illegal, unreported, and unregulated fishing both within areas of U.S. jurisdiction and on the high seas. I ask that my written statement be submitted for the record.

Senator MARKEY. Without objection, so ordered.

Admiral KENNEY. Before I begin, on behalf of the Commandant I would like to thank the members of the committee for their support in passing the Consolidated Appropriations Act of 2014. This act will help relieve the erosive effects of sequestration on the Coast Guard. It will restore frontline operations, such as fisheries enforcement, and badly needed training hours. It will ease many of the personnel management restrictions we have faced over the past year.

Safeguarding living marine resources is a longstanding Coast Guard mission and it remains a vital U.S. economic interest today. The Coast Guard embraces its role as the principal Federal at-sea enforcement agency for the protection of living marine resources within the U.S. EEZ and on the high seas. The Coast Guard supports the State Department and NOAA in their efforts to combat IUU fishing. Actors engaged in this illicit activity often exploit the gaps between governance structures and operate in areas where there is little or no effective enforcement presence.

The four international treaties under consideration by the committee will significantly shrink those areas most vulnerable to IUU fishing and will enhance the Coast Guard's ability to provide at-sea enforcement for the conservation of precious living marine resources.

Since 2008, the Coast Guard has conducted over 100 high seas boardings and issued violations to over 20 vessels. These enforcement efforts enabled recent seizures of stateless vessels, such as the fishing vessel *DA CHENG* and its illegally taken catch from high seas driftnet fishing. Notably, the Coast Guard cooperated closely with Chinese officials to turn over the vessel, crew, and catch for Chinese enforcement efforts, which resulted in forfeiture of the catch, destruction of the IUU vessel, and a significant fine for the master.

The Northwest Atlantic Fisheries Organization Convention Amendment will help to align treaty activities with contemporary enforcement practices within the convention area. Both the North Pacific and South Pacific conventions will establish a modern governance mechanism to provide a stronger at-sea enforcement regime on the high seas of the Pacific Ocean. The Port State Measures Agreement will address illegal fishing activity by establishing economic disincentives for those who violate the law.

Together, these four treaties will facilitate joint efforts between the Coast Guard, NOAA, the State Department, and our international partners to preserve and protect valuable living marine resources that are critical to the United States and world economies.

These treaties and other international instruments that address fisheries governance also have a secondary benefit of facilitating efforts to identify and counter other maritime security threats. Groups or individuals involved in illegal fishing may also be engaged in other crimes. In carrying out the provision of these treaties, the Coast Guard can promote maritime governments and increase maritime domain awareness on the high seas, thus enabling the service to respond to a range of transnational threats.

Enforcement of both the outer reaches of the U.S. EEZ and international fisheries management schemes is largely a mission conducted by Coast Guard offshore assets. The Coast Guard remains steadfast in its commitment to recapitalizing its offshore fleet to ensure it is capable of addressing these threats, such as illegal fishing on the high seas and in our sovereign waters.

The capabilities of new assets, such as the National Security Cutter, one of which is on patrol in the Pacific as I speak, and the Offshore Patrol Cutter, which is in the preliminary and contract design phase, will maintain our ability to conduct Coast Guard missions in the distant reaches of the U.S. EEZ and on the high seas. These replacement platforms for our aging offshore fleet, some of which are nearly 50 years old, will make the Coast Guard better able to close those awareness and presence gaps that allow IUU fishing to occur undetected.

In conclusion, the Coast Guard strongly supports these four international fisheries treaties. We will continue to work closely with the State Department, NOAA, and our international partners to achieve national and international objectives to address IUU fishing. Such cooperation is a critical step in sustaining marine ecosystems worldwide and to address threats that impact the U.S. economy and global food security.

Thank you for the opportunity to testify before you today. I would be happy to answer any questions you may have.

[The prepared statement of Admiral Kenney follows:]

PREPARED STATEMENT OF REAR ADMIRAL FREDERICK J. KENNEY

Good afternoon, Chairman Markey, Ranking Member Rubio, and distinguished members of the committee. It is a pleasure to appear before you today in support of four international fisheries agreements that will improve the Coast Guard's ability to deter, prevent, and enforce rules against Illegal, Unregulated, and Unreported (IUU) fishing both within areas of U.S. jurisdiction and on the high seas.

Safeguarding living marine resources is a longstanding Coast Guard mission and it remains a vital U.S. economic interest today. Beginning with 19th century protection of the Bering Sea fur seal herds and continuing through the post-World War II expansion in the size and efficiency of global fishing fleets, the Coast Guard has embraced its role as the principal, federal, on-scene law enforcement agency for the protection of U.S. living marine resources. Today, the Coast Guard maintains a law enforcement presence within the U.S. Exclusive Economic Zone (EEZ), which is the largest in the world.

IUU fishing activity is global in reach, and it adversely affects marine ecosystems by distorting competition and jeopardizing the economic survival of coastal communities whose livelihoods depend upon local fisheries. The Coast Guard supports the State Department and the National Oceanic and Atmospheric Administration (NOAA) in their efforts to combat IUU. Actors engaged in IUU fishing often exploit the gaps between governance structures and operate in areas where there is little or no effective enforcement presence. These four international fisheries agreements will significantly shrink those gaps utilized by IUU fishing and will improve the United States deterrence efforts, thus promoting the optimal management and protection of vital living marine resources and their environments.

Coast Guard efforts to deter and combat IUU fishing span both domestic and internationalfisheries, and they bridge the Service's maritime security and maritime stewardship goals.

These goals, outlined in the "U.S. Coast Guard Strategy for Maritime Safety, Security, and Stewardship," are driven by national policy including "Presidential Decision Directive 36: Protecting the Ocean Environment," laws such as the Magnuson-Stevens Fishery Conservation and Management Act, and international ocean governance structures, such as U.S. membership within international Regional Fishery Management Organizations (RFMOs). Each of the four fisheries agreements being considered by the Senate will enhance the Coast Guard's ability to provide at-sea enforcement for the conservation and management of living marine resources and their environments.

Effective enforcement requires a clear understanding of the Northwest Atlantic Fisheries Organization (NAFO) Convention's goals and objectives. The NAFO Convention Amendment accomplishes this through modernization of the Convention text that has been in force since 1979. The changes will help align Coast Guard enforcement with contemporary practices within the Convention area.

The North and South Pacific Conventions will establish a modern governance mechanism that will enable a stronger at-sea enforcement regime on the high seas of the Pacific and facilitate more effective Coast Guard enforcement efforts in the region. To further achieve this goal, the Coast Guard will continue to work closely with the State Department and NOAA to ensure the conventions include a high-seas boarding and inspection regime in line with Articles 21 and 22 of the 1995 U.N. Fish Stock Agreement.

The Port State Measures Agreement is another tool to combat IUU fishing by addressing the problem through economic disincentives. Without access to ports of convenience, vessels engaged in IUU fishing will be unable to sell their product or receive logistical support for operations. Forcing these vessels into ports further away from commerce centers and fishing grounds will increase their operating costs and diminish economic gains for illegally caught fish or fish product. Limiting the ports available to these vessels would also simplify enforcement by targeting investigations of illicit activity in ports known to support IUU fishing.

Regional Fishery Management Organizations (RFMOs) have proven to be highly effective in managing fisheries resources beyond areas of national jurisdiction. For example, the Western and Central Pacific Fisheries Commission (WCPFC), one of the first in the world to employ a fully developed boarding and inspection protocol for high seas enforcement based on the U.N. Fish Stocks Agreement, has produced a level of governance and cooperation for long-term resource management that was previously not feasible. The Coast Guard is proud to have been involved in its development and negotiation, and as a leader in its enforcement. Under the WCPFC since 2008, the Coast Guard has conducted over 100 high seas boardings and inspections, issuing violations to over 20 vessels. Likewise, Coast Guard cutter patrols in support of these enforcement efforts have also enabled recent seizures of stateless vessels such as the fishing vessel *DA CHENG* and its illegally taken catch resulting from high-seas drift-net fishing. Notably, the Coast Guard cooperated closely with Chinese officials to turn over the vessel, crew, and catch for Chinese enforcement efforts. The Coast Guard looks forward to continuing to provide leadership in the global fight against IUU fishing in these new RFMOs.

Enforcement at the outer reaches of the U.S. EEZ and within high-sea areas managed by RFMOs is a mission largely conducted by Coast Guard off-shore assets. Cutter transit to most of the eight noncontiguous U.S. EEZs in the Western and Central Pacific takes several days (and more than a week in some cases) from the nearest Coast Guard facility. The Coast Guard's offshore recapitalization program ensures that these critical missions will have the organic capabilities necessary to meet the extreme demands of time, distance, and weather these operations entail.

As a secondary benefit, carrying out the provisions of these Conventions enables the Coast Guard to increase Maritime Domain Awareness on the high seas and more effectively respond to a range of transnational threats.

In conclusion, the Coast Guard strongly supports these four international fisheries agreements and will continue to work closely with the State Department, NOAA, and our international partners to achieve national and international objectives for managing sustainable fisheries worldwide and to address IUU fishing. The world's oceans are truly a global commons, requiring a global approach toward their conservation and management. In the face of an increasing need for food security and the increasing scarcity of marine resources, the U.S. Coast Guard stands ready to confront IUU fishing to preserve the long-term viability of migratory fish stocks that affect U.S. fisheries.

Thank you for the opportunity to testify before you today. I would be happy to answer any questions you may have.

Senator MARKEY. Thank you, Admiral, very much. Again, we thank all of the witnesses.

Another rollcall has gone off on the Senate floor, so we will have to once again stand in a brief recess.

[Recess from 3:23 p.m. to 3:43 p.m.]

Senator MARKEY. The committee will reconvene and the Chair will recognize himself for a round of questions.

Mr. Smith, the United States is already a member of a number of regional fisheries management organizations. Can you provide examples of how membership in those organizations has benefited U.S. fisheries?

Mr. SMITH. Thank you, Senator Markey. You are correct, we are a member of a number of regional fisheries management organizations and we have seen that our work within those organizations has directly benefited our fisheries, including for example the swordfish fishery in the North Atlantic, a fishery that was in great trouble not too long ago. It was overfished and subject to overfishing. The stock had crashed. The United States had taken some steps to better manage the fishery, to close some areas, to do some things to help the fishery recover.

But our taking those actions alone would not be sufficient because other countries were fishing on the same stocks. We were able to go to ICAT, the International Convention for the Conservation of Atlantic Tuna, and we were able to work with them to develop management measures that have worked, have resulted in the application of quotas that are science-based and precautionary, the application of other management measures that have led to the stock now having recovered, being managed in a fully sustainable fashion, and allowing our fleet to rely on it as an important source of fish for our markets and for our food security.

Senator MARKEY. Thank you.

Admiral Kenney, the Coast Guard is already taking steps to combat illegal fishing in both the United States EEZ and on the high seas. For example, in seizing the fishing vessel *DA CHENG* the Coast Guard found 30 metric tons of albacore tuna and 6 metric tons of shark fins and bodies. What role do you see these treaties playing in enhancing your ability to do your work?

Admiral KENNEY. Thank you for that question, Mr. Chairman. These treaties will enhance the Coast Guard's ability to detect and enforce IUU fishing laws, regulations, and treaties. Under the NAFO amendments, the Coast Guard will be able to continue conducting joint patrols with the Canadian Department of Fisheries and Oceans, as we do. For example, in 2012 we conducted the very successful Operation Nanook with the Canadians, which did result in some boardings, although no violations were found.

The Port State Measures Agreement will enable us to work closely with NOAA to prevent IUU fishing vessels from entering U.S. ports. The Coast Guard can add to that effort significantly through our Advanced Notice of Arrival System and allow NOAA to take action as vessels enter port.

With respect to the North Pacific and South Pacific treaties, allowing the Coast Guard to have presence and domain awareness in these areas will also allow us to take effective enforcement action. A good example of that type of cooperative effort is the Oceana Maritime Security Initiative, which is an initiative that is led by the U.S. Pacific Command and has allowed Coast Guard boarding teams to ride along U.S. naval vessels to conduct fisheries boardings in conjunction with Pacific Island nations to help them preserve their fish stocks.

Senator MARKEY. Thank you.

Ambassador Balton, developing nations are impacted by illegal fishing in a number of ways. Somalia, for example, loses $300 million a year because of illegal fishing. In addition to direct economic impacts, many developing nations depend on fisheries products for subsistence purposes. How will these agreements help to address the impact of illegal fishing and environmental degradation on developing nations?

Ambassador BALTON. Thank you, Mr. Chairman. You are exactly right, developing countries bear the brunt of the problem with respect to IUU fishing. I would note that for the Port State Measures Agreement a number of them have already ratified, recognizing that that instrument will help them. I will mention now: Angola, Benin, Brazil, Ghana, Indonesia, Kenya, Mozambique, Peru, Samoa, Sierra Leone, among others.

The Port State Measures Agreement is a great example of a cooperative effort to crack down on IUU fishing. It is cost effective. It would also allow us and other developed countries and multilateral donors to provide assistance to developing countries to help them implement relatively inexpensive measures in port to prevent illegally harvested fish from being offloaded there.

The other agreements, too, by cracking down on IUU fishing and having science-based management should allow for sustainability of fisheries, also to the betterment of the economy of developing countries.

Senator MARKEY. Thank you.

We thank each of the witnesses for your expert testimony. It is going to go a long way toward our ability to be able to move this treaty through the committee and out onto the Senate floor. We thank you for all of your excellent work.

Now I would ask the second panel to please come up and sit in front of your names. Then we will begin the testimony.

[Pause.]

Senator MARKEY. Our final panel will illustrate some of the real world consequences of illegal fishing. I will briefly introduce our witnesses and then we can hear their testimony.

Captain Ray Kane is the outreach coordinator for the Cape Cod Commercial Fishermen's Alliance. He is the owner and operator of F/V FRENZY and has been a Cape Cod fishermen for nearly 40 years.

Mark Gleason is the executive director of the Alaska Bering Sea Crabbers, an association of crab fishermen, primarily based out of Alaska, Washington, and Oregon.

Ambassador Mark Lagon is global politics and security chair at the Master of Science in Foreign Service Program at Georgetown University and adjunct senior fellow for Human Rights at the Council on Foreign Relations. He was an Ambassador at Large and directed the U.S. Department of State Office to Monitor and Combat Trafficking in Persons from 2007 to 2009, and he is, most importantly, a former member of the staff of this committee, and I am told also a native of Massachusetts. So we are keeping the panels balanced in that sense.

So we will begin with you, Mr. Kane. Whenever you are ready, please begin.

STATEMENT OF RAYMOND KANE, OUTREACH COORDINATOR, CAPE COD FISHERMEN'S ALLIANCE, CHATHAM, MA

Mr. KANE. Good afternoon, Chairman Markey. My name is Capt. Ray Kane. I appreciate your invitation to testify at this important hearing. By way of background, I have been actively involved in the Massachusetts commercial fishing industry for over 40 years, and I have participated in virtually every New England fishery, including tuna, lobster, scallops, and groundfish.

In addition to being the owner and operator of the fishing vessel *FRENZY,* I also serve as the Fishery Advocate for the Cape Code

Commercial Fishermen's Alliance. Today I am testifying on behalf of the hardworking small boat fishermen from both Cape Cod and the islands. That comprises the alliance.

As an organization dedicated to sustainable fisheries, we support the establishment and strengthening of effective regional fisheries management organizations, also known as RFMOs. Effective multi-lateral RFMOs are the only way to manage and conserve fisheries on the high seas and as such we firmly support their creation in the North and South Pacific Ocean.

Because our Cape Cod fishermen are not involved in the Pacific fisheries, nor do they fish in the NAFO area, my testimony today will focus on the Port State Measures Agreement aimed at deter-ring and eliminating illegal, unreported, and unregulated fishing, referred to as "IUU fishing." IUU fishing is a multibillion dollar in-dustry, and it is growing. IUU fishing is fueled by the overall in-crease in fish prices and dwindling global fish stocks. Recent stud-ies suggest that foreign illegal fishing is a worldwide business that accounts for up to $23.5 billion worth of seafood annually, or 25 million tons of fish and, even better, Senator Markey, six times more fish than the entire U.S. commercial fishing industry annual landings.

The Port State Measures Agreement is built on the promise that IUU fishing can be reduced if IUU fish can be prevented from en-tering the global commerce. The most effective way of accom-plishing this is to make it extremely difficult for IUU fish to be offloaded in a port. In this regard, the agreement establishes the first global standards to control port access from foreign fishing vessels that engage in IUU fishing. These standards include man-dating parties, port states, to require prior notice of a foreign fish-ing vessel's arrival in their port, restricting port entry and services to foreign vessels known or suspected of IUU fishing, adopting min-imum dockside inspection and training standards, and the sharing of information about IUU vessels with the appropriate RFMOs.

But what is most critical about the agreement is that it creates an obligation of the signatory nations to apply and implement these measures. In other words, these measures are to be enforce-able, not merely aspirational. The truth is many coastal nations are simply not as rigorous in their enforcement as is the United States. What is worse is that it is widely understood that around the world the illegal sale of additional fish quotas and fishing li-censes is extremely lucrative, which fuels the IUU epidemic.

So why is this agreement important to the small day boat fisher-men on Cape Cod, my fellow fishermen from Gloucester, Boston, New Bedford, and all the New England coast, and for that matter the entire East Coast? The answer is simple. For too many years, New England fishermen have sacrificed to rebuild highly migratory stocks while foreign fishermen engaged in IUU fishing are reaping the benefits of our efforts by targeting those very same fish. This is particularly true for tuna and swordfish fishermen along the New England coast.

Mr. Chairman, American fishermen and especially Massachu-setts fishermen have had enough of IUU fishing. We need to level the playing field in order to make sure that we have an equal foot-ing in the marketplace and to ensure that our conservation efforts and sacrifices are not undone by IUU fishing. We believe the Port State Measures Agreement is a good place to start and we strongly encourage this committee and the entire Senate to approve the agreement as soon as possible.

Thank you and I would be happy to answer any questions.

[The prepared statement of Mr. Kane follows:]

PREPARED STATEMENT OF CAPT. RAYMOND KANE

Good afternoon, Senators Markey and Rubio. My name is Captain Ray Kane and I appreciate your invitation to testify at this important hearing. By way of background, I have been actively involved in the Massachusetts commercial fishing industry for over 40 years, and I have participated in virtually every fishery including tuna, lobster, scallops, and groundfish. In addition to being the owner and operator of the F/V Frenzy, I also serve as the fishery advocate for the Cape Cod Commercial Fishermen's Alliance (Alliance). Today I am testifying on behalf of the hard working, small boat fishermen from Cape Cod and the Islands that comprise the Alliance.

The subject of today's hearing is the consideration of four fisheries agreements including an Amendment to the Convention of Future Multilateral Cooperation in the Northwest Atlantic (NAFO); the Convention on the Conservation and Management of High Seas Fisheries Resources in the North Pacific Ocean; the Convention on the Conservation and Management of High Seas Fishery Resources in the South Pacific Ocean (SPRFMO); and the Agreement on Port State Measures to Prevent, Deter, and Eliminate Illegal, Unreported, and Unregulated Fishing (PSMA).

As an organization dedicated to sustainable fisheries, we support the establishment and strengthening of effective regional fishery management organizations, also known as RFMOs. RFMOs for high-seas areas are especially important as by their very nature, high-seas areas are under the control of no one single nation. As we painfully learned from high-seas fishing in the Northwest Atlantic Ocean, when there are no rules and no enforcement, there is also no conservation. Effective multilateral RFMO's are the only way to manage and conserve fisheries on the high seas and as such we firmly support their creation in the North and South Pacific Ocean. Because our Cape Cod fishermen are not involved in the Pacific fisheries nor do they fish in the NAFO area, my testimony today will focus on the Port State Measures Agreement aimed at deterring and eliminating IUU fishing.

Make no mistake about it. Illegal, unreported and unregulated fishing—IUU fishing—is a multibillion dollar industry and it is growing. IUU fishing is fueled by the overall increase in fish prices and dwindling global fish stocks. Recent studies suggest that foreign illegal fishing is a worldwide business that accounts for up to $23.5 billion worth of seafood annually, or 26 million tons of fish—six times more fish than the entire U.S. commercial fishing industry annual catch. Some of the biggest culprits involve fishing vessels flagged from EU and Asian nations including Korean, Taiwan, and China. Recent research by Daniel Pauly, a scientist at the University of British Columbia, found that even though China claims to have the biggest distant-water fishing fleet in the world, it only reported 386,000 tons of fish caught per year between 2000 and 2011. This same research also estimated China was catching more than 12 times the amount of fish it reported.

The United States has been a global leader in fighting IUU fishing. Domestically, we have some of the strongest laws aimed at curtailing IUU fishing and ensuring that IUU fish does not enter our markets. Under the High Seas Driftnet Fishing Moratorium Protection Act, as amended, the United States lists nations identified as having vessels engaged in IUU fishing and can both deny port privileges to IUU vessels and prohibit the import of fish products from IUU nations into the U.S. Additionally, the Magnuson-Stevens Act includes some of the strictest enforcement measures and penalties to deter U.S. fishermen from engaging in IUU fishing. Believe me, the United States Coast Guard, the National Marine Fisheries Service and the Department of Homeland Security do an excellent job enforcing a whole suite of conservation, safety, and security laws on American fishermen.

Internationally, the U.S. has also taken a leadership role. Through the various RFMOs, the United States has pushed for stronger measures to deter and detect IUU fishing, including adoption of IUU vessel lists, market-related measures, vessel monitoring and surveillance programs and prohibiting the transfer of catch at sea. Unfortunately, as is the case with most international fishery organizations, application and enforcement of these measures remains mixed at best.

The Port State Measures Agreement is built on the premise that IUU fishing can be reduced if IUU fish can be prevented from entering global commerce, and the most effective way of accomplishing this is to make it extremely difficult for IUU fish to be offloaded in a port. In this regard, the Agreement establishes the first global standards to control port access from foreign illegal fishing vessels that engage in IUU fishing. These standards include mandating parties (port states) to require prior notice of a foreign fishing vessel's arrival in their port, restricting port entry and port services to foreign vessels known or suspected of IUU fishing, adopting minimum dockside inspection and training standards, and the sharing of information about IUU vessels with the appropriate RFMOs. But what is most critical about the Agreement is that it creates an obligation of the signatory nations to apply and implement these measures; in other words, these measures are to be enforceable, not merely aspirational. The truth is, many coastal nations are simply not as rigorous in their enforcement as the United States. What's worse is that it is widely understood that around the world the illegal sale of additional fish quotas and fishing licenses is extremely lucrative which fuels the IUU epidemic.

So why is this Agreement important to the small, day boat fishermen on Cape Cod and, for that matter, my fellow fishermen from Gloucester, Boston, New Bedford, and all along the New England coast? The answer is simple: for too many years, New England fishermen have sacrificed to rebuild highly migratory stocks, while foreign fishermen engaged in IUU fishing reap the benefits of our efforts by targeting those very same fish. This is particularly true for tuna and swordfish fishermen along the New England coast.

For decades, Atlantic tuna and swordfish quotas for American fishermen were significantly reduced for conservation reasons while foreign IUU fishing persisted and undermined those attempts at sustainability. Unlike inshore fish stocks where the United States can exert effective unilateral management within our 200 mile exclusive economic zone, highly migratory stocks like tuna and swordfish swim throughout the Atlantic Ocean and are therefore susceptible to overexploitation by foreign fishermen in international waters. In addition to undermining conservation efforts, IUU fish depresses the market for American harvested fish both in terms of demand and price. In sum, IUU fish undermines our businesses as well as our stock rebuilding efforts. Thus, our fishermen feel the double whammy: fish that we abstain from harvesting to ensure a sustainable stock are harvested instead through IUU fishing, and yet when we do harvest our quota, the markets and prices for our fish are depressed because of the presence of IUU fish in the marketplace.

Mr. Chairman, American fishermen and especially Massachusetts fishermen have had enough of IUU fishing! We need to level the playing field in order to make sure that we have an equal footing in the marketplace and to ensure that our conservation efforts and sacrifices are not undone by IUU fishing. We believe the Port State Measures Agreement is a good place to start and we strongly encourage this committee and the entire Senate to approve the Agreement as soon as possible.

Senator MARKEY. And what high school did you go to?

Mr. KANE. Actually, I grew up in Yonkers, NY, Senator, Yonkers.

Senator MARKEY. I can hear that. I can hear it.

Mr. KANE. But I am a wash-ashore and I have been fishing since I have been 23, post-college.

Senator MARKEY. Thank you.

What high school did you go to, Ambassador?

Ambassador LAGON. I went to Middlesex School in Concord.

Senator MARKEY. Right in Concord, beautiful. Welcome, Ambassador. Whenever you are ready, please begin.

STATEMENT OF HON. MARK P. LAGON, GLOBAL POLITICS AND SECURITY CHAIR, MASTER OF SCIENCE IN FOREIGN SERVICE PROGRAM, GEORGETOWN UNIVERSITY, AND ADJUNCT SENIOR FELLOW FOR HUMAN RIGHTS, COUNCIL ON FOREIGN RELATIONS, WASHINGTON, DC

Ambassador LAGON Great. Chairman Markey, it is a privilege to testify here. I did serve the committee as a staffer. It is great to be back. The committee also supported my confirmation to become Ambassador at Large to combat human trafficking.

Somewhat more recently, I have become an uncompensated board member of something called the Global Business Coalition Against Human Trafficking, that includes some star players like

Coca-Cola, Delta, Ford, Hilton, and Microsoft. They, as a coalition, try to promote measures to shut windows of vulnerability to human trafficking that taint vital and legitimate business, like some of the measures I want to talk about today, if I might.

I would like to speak on how human trafficking, netting people, is intermingled with IUU fishing. I would ask that my written testimony be entered into the record, please.

Increasingly, evidence indicates that labor and even sexual exploitation occurs on fishing vessels that exists largely unnoticed. In 2013 the Maritime Labor Convention came into force to protect the rights of those working on merchant and passenger ships, but unfortunately no comparable legal measures exist for workers' rights on fishing vessels. Fishing vessels are exempt from safety standards and monitoring requirements of the International Maritime Organization.

So fishing vessels of all sizes are regulated solely by the country from which they are registered, or, the "flag" state, rather than "port" states where they bring in their cargo and would be more likely to get caught doing something illegal. This all amounts to a kind of governance "black hole." Leading observers in our society, like the Pew Charitable Trusts, with great expertise on IUU and enforcement challenges, have been focused on exposing this weak regulatory environment.

It impacts a global fishing industry where the annual revenues are somewhere between $80 and $85 billion, and that industry is trying to meet increasing demand for seafood. That context creates an opportunity for human traffickers to seek maximum gain with little risk.

I would like to quote a 2011 U.N. Office on Drugs and Crime report on this territory. It said: "The most disturbing finding about IUU fishing was the severity of the abuse of fishers trafficked for the purpose of forced labor. It is cruel and inhuman treatment in the extreme. Disturbing in particular is the frequency of trafficking in children."

So let us take a particular example. Thailand's fishing fleet is chronically short on fishermen, short by maybe 60,000 fishermen a year, and foreign labor makes up 40 percent of that gap. Traffickers travel inland in countries like Cambodia and Myanmar and recruit men who, with the help of corrupt border police, get sold into bondage at sea.

Some texture comes from an NPR story in 2012 that followed a man named Vannak Prum. He looked for a fishing job to help pay for his pregnant wife's hospital bills and was sold to a Thai fishing vessel, subject to 20-hour work days in dangerous and unsanitary conditions, and was held without pay for 3 years at sea, including fishing illegally in Indonesian waters.

A 2009 survey by the U.N. found that 59 percent of migrants trafficked aboard Thai fishing vessels witnessed the murder of a fellow worker. A nonprofit in 2013 interviewed 14 men from Myanmar rescued from Thai fishing vessels and they reported seeing beatings, a crew member tortured or executed, and 5 murdered. In 2013 150 Cambodian and Burmese victims were rescued from Thai fishing vessels.

But it is not just in that region of the world. The State Department's Trafficking in Persons Report links trafficking to the fishing industry in numerous examples—including women and children trafficked for prostitution—in places across the Pacific, Asia, and Africa. A nonprofit actually indicated evidence in 2013 that a fishing firm in Sierra Leone was trafficking girls for sex purposes.

The U.S. fishing fleet is highly compliant with domestic and international laws, while illegal fishing by foreign vessels poses real problems for the United States, particularly along the U.S.-Mexico border, where there has been a drastic increase of incursions of illegal Mexican fishing vessels. Recent reports suggest that these same vessels are used to smuggle drugs and humans from Northeast Mexico into Texas.

So the Port State Measures Agreement will strengthen port inspections, enhance communications, and deny port entry to illegal fishing vessels. It is cost effective, has an enforcement mechanism, and is going to increase the cost to illegal fishing operations. Increasing accountability and economic incentives brought about by the PSMA would help erode various criminal activities associated with illegal fishing, including human trafficking.

Twenty-five nations need to ratify the PSMA to come into force and the world is waiting for the United States to act as an example.

The Trafficking Victims Protection Act, to conclude, was reauthorized in March 2013 with strong bipartisan support, bipartisan support as strong as I witnessed as a Senate Foreign Relations Committee staffer responsible for helping move through the original legislation in 2000. The PSMA complements that law and institutes standards consistent with already existing U.S. practice and can pay big dividends through enhanced accountability.

I strongly urge the Senate to ratify and implement it and send a message to the world that it will not tolerate either illegal fishing or gross human rights abuses. All the treaties and agreements under consideration today would shed sunshine on illegal fishing. They would advance the stewardship of marine ecosystems. They would advance fairness to businesses playing by the rules, as reflected by my fellow panelists. But they would also prevent vulnerable people from being utterly dehumanized, violated, and even killed at sea.

Thank you for inviting me.

[The prepared statement of Ambassador Lagon follows:]

PREPARED STATEMENT OF AMBASSADOR MARK P. LAGON

Chairman Markey, Senator Rubio, members of the committee, it is a privilege to testify here. I served at the committee as a staffer, assisting then Senator Sam Brownback and the late Senator Paul Wellstone in finalizing the Trafficking Victims Protection Act of 2000. The committee 7 years later supported my confirmation to serve as Ambassdor at Large directing the Office to Monitor and Combat Trafficking in Persons the Act created, where I named the State Department's annual award for the U.S. bilateral ambassador doing the most to combat trafficking after Senator Wellstone.

Thereafter, I became CEO of the leading U.S. antitrafficking nonprofit, Polaris Project, and in 2012 Founding Board Member (uncompensated, to be clear) of the Global Business Coalition Against Human Trafficking (gbcat.org), which includes Carlson, Coca Cola, Delta Airlines, Ford Motor Company, Hilton Hotels, Microsoft, and NXP Semiconductor among its members. This coalition of thought leaders promotes best practices to shut the windows of vulnerability to human trafficking tainting vital, legitimate business—through means like those I will recommend today.

My tenure from 2007 to 2009 as Ambassador at Large involved rebalancing the focus on human trafficking toward that based on exploitation for labor—in addition to that horrifically based on commoditized sex. Labor trafficking is a broader phenomenon, yet still prosecuted today globally less than one-sixth as often as sex trafficking, according to the 2013 Department of State "Trafficking in Persons Report." [1] That tenure also witnessed the revelation of how often human trafficking occurs in the seafood sector—from the victims of forced labor in seafood processing I met in Thailand in 2007, to boys fishing in Ghana's Lake Volta so vividly depicted in the documentary film on child trafficking, "Not My Life," [2] which we at the State Department Office lent advice to get made.

The focus of today's hearing is on illegal, unreported and unregulated (IUU) fishing, the Port States Measures Agreement (PSMA), as well as three other international fisheries agreements. My testimony will center on human trafficking as it relates to fishing vessels and illegal fishing worldwide. I ask that my written testimony please be entered into the hearing record.

It is important to state from the outset that there is limited information available on the relationship between illegal fishing, human trafficking, and other criminal activities. These activities can occur independently. Obviously only some fishing vessels are engaged in illegal fishing, and human trafficking. However, the available data suggests that the confluence of these activities at sea does occur all too often, requiring a strong response from the United States. These illicit activities impact economically disadvantaged and vulnerable people, global commerce, and the health of our ocean environment, and merits your action. I strongly urge this committee to support and advance the Port States Measures Agreement in particular as soon as possible.

Human trafficking is not limited to activities on land, and increasingly evidence indicates that labor and even sexual exploitation are occurring at sea, and particularly on fishing vessels that exist largely unnoticed by the rest of the world. In 2013, the Maritime Labor Convention (MLC) came into force to protect the rights of seafarers on merchant vessels and passenger ships, but unfortunately, no comparable legal measures exist for workers rights aboard fishing vessels worldwide. Further, fishing vessels are generally exempt from the vessel safety standards and monitoring requirements of the International Maritime Organization (IMO). As a result, a range of fishing vessels of all sizes and seaworthiness are regulated solely by the country from which the vessel is registered, the vessel's "flag" state, and they can operate across wide swaths of the ocean for months or years at a time with relative autonomy. Enforcement actions have traditionally been left to the states where the boats are registered, or "flagged," rather than the "port" states where they bring their cargo to shore, where they would be more likely to be caught doing something illegal.

Moreover, fishing boats are much less carefully regulated than other ships. Because fishing vessels are not required to have identification numbers, enormous ships are known to change names and flags of registration to stay a step ahead of authorities. Interpol issued two worldwide alerts last year for vessels that had done just that.[3] Fishing vessels are not required to carry satellite transponders, which makes it easy for them to evade surveillance. This all amounts to a governance "black hole."

This weak regulatory environment impacts a global fishing industry with annual revenues of $80–$85 billion that seeks to meet the increasing demand for seafood.[4] These financial and regulatory conditions create an opportunity for traffickers to seize maximum gain with little risk, at the expense of fellow human beings who they in effect enslave. A 2011 report of the United Nations Office on Drugs and Crime (UNODC), "Transnational Organized Crime in the Fishing Industry," concluded: "Perhaps the most disturbing finding of the study was the severity of the abuse of fishers trafficked for the purpose of forced labour on board fishing vessels. These practices can only be described as cruel and inhumane treatment in the extreme . . . A particularly disturbing facet of this form of exploitation is the frequency of trafficking in children in the fishing industry." [5]

We lack robust statistics of the full extent of human trafficking abuses associated with the global fishing industry, but a growing list of examples highlights the severity of the problem. Bloomberg Businessweek conducted a 6-month investigation into debt bondage schemes in Indonesia where men, desperate for work, were exploited on Korean-flagged fishing vessels operating off the coast of New Zealand. Fishing company agents rushed men into signing misleading contracts that allowed the fishing company to withhold salaries, and they collected collateral assets from workers' families. Further, crewmembers were required to work to the company's loosely defined ''satisfaction,'' or be sent home without pay and charged $1,000 for airfare.[6] Though the crew lived in cramped, unsanitary conditions with the daily threat of physical violence and rape, the contract terms assessed fines for any worker who ran away from the job. Workers were forced to work, knowing their families would ultimately be held responsible.

A 2011 report from the International Organization for Migration (IOM) entitled ''Trafficking of Fishermen in Thailand'' provides detailed information on the scale and scope of the human trafficking in the Thai fishing industry.[7] Citizens of Southeast Asian countries are subjected to human trafficking on Thai vessels that fish on longer voyages in foreign waters far from enforcement (as compared to vessels that fish in their exclusive economic zone, or EEZ, waters and return to port frequently). Workers are vulnerable due to their limited potential to leave the ship. In 2012, National Public Radio produced a special report[8] exposing significant human trafficking of men from Cambodia and Myanmar on Thai fishing vessels. Thailand has a large fishing fleet but is chronically short on fishermen—short by up to 60,000 per year—and foreign labor makes up 40 percent of the men working at sea. The report indicates that human traffickers travel inland to remote villages in Cambodia and Myanmar and recruit men who they move with the complicity of corrupt border police to be sold into bondage at sea.

The NPR story follows a man named Vannak Prum as he looked for a short-term fishing job to pay for his pregnant wife's hospital bills, but was sold to a Thai fishing vessel, subject to 20-hour work days in dangerous and unsanitary conditions, and held without pay for 3 years at sea. Prum's account documents illegal fishing inside of Indonesian waters and his vessel evading gunfire before slipping into Malaysian waters. Prum eventually escaped by jumping overboard while fishing near an island off Malaysia, but once ashore, he was sold into indentured servitude on a palm oil plantation by a local police officer. This case reflects archetypical human trafficking: vulnerable groups of people robbed of their autonomy because they lack any access to justice.

Fishermen trapped at sea are subjected to violent, and sometimes deadly, abuse while aboard Thai vessels. A 2009 survey by the United Nations Inter-Agency Project on Human Trafficking (UNIAP) found that 59 percent of interviewed migrants trafficked aboard Thai fishing boats reported witnessing the murder of a fellow worker.[9] Accidents, dangerous working conditions and the fear of being physically abused are common, but reports suggest that most vessels had little to no medical supplies and would not stop work to seek medical attention for the crew.[10] In 2013, the Environmental Justice Foundation (EJF) interviewed 14 Myanmar men rescued from Thai fishing vessels who reported beatings by the senior crew, and in two cases, the victims reported seeing a fellow crewmember tortured and executed for trying to escape, as well as the murder of five others.[11] Further, EJF interviews with rescued victims confirmed that the vessels often fished illegally in foreign waters.[12] In 2013, 150 Cambodian and Burmese victims were rescued from Thai fishing vessels in ports around the world, but the U.S. State Department reports that this is likely only a fraction of the total number of Asian men victimized by trafficking on fishing boats.[13]

The State Department's ''Trafficking in Persons Report for 2013'' suggests that the connection between human trafficking and the fishing industry is not limited to Thailand, and there are numerous examples involving victims—including woman and children trafficked for prostitution—from poor and developing countries across the Pacific, Asia, and Africa.[14] In July 2013, a humanitarian organization reported that a foreign fishing firm based in Sierra Leone trafficked girls for purposes of sex, leaving port with the girls onboard before they were rescued by the local authorities.[15] Many other woman and children are not as fortunate.

The same circumstances that make fishing vessels opportune for human trafficking also make them susceptible to other forms of transnational organized crime, including drug trafficking. For instance, a State Department report notes that drug smuggling is often aided by fishing boats moving drugs through the Bahamas, Jamaica, and Florida.[16] The 2011 UNODC report Transnational Organized Crime in the Fishing Industry that I previously mentioned addressed the extent to which criminal activities within the fishing industry were a threat to the law-abiding and legitimate fishing industry, local fishing communities, and the public at large. The study confirmed labor abuses aboard fishing vessels, as well as the links between illegal fishing, and transnational organized crime, and drug trafficking. Specifically, it found that fishing vessels are used for smuggling migrants, drugs (primarily cocaine), and weapons, and committing acts of terrorism. Fishing vessels are used as ''mother ships'' serving as base stations from which criminal activities are coordinated, as supply vessels for other vessels engaged in criminal activities, or simply as cover for clandestine activities at sea and in port. The study also found that some transnational fishing operators are engaged in marine living resource crime. These fishing operations are highly sophisticated and employ complex incorporation and vessel registration strategies to avoid tracking. They coordinate at-sea vessel support services to aid in moving illegally caught fish to market, often supported by fraudulent catch documentation.[17]

As stated at the outset, the data that explicitly connects illegal fishing, human trafficking, and other criminal activities is limited, but mounting evidence suggests that fishing vessels engaged in one of these illicit activities are likely to also engage in the others. There is evidence of widespread IUU fishing occurring in the Asia-Pacific region, estimated at 3.4–8.1 million tons per year,[18] costing countries in that region significant annual revenue losses (losses estimated, for instance, at $2.5 billion in 2007[19]) and resulting in overexploited fisheries. The presence of IUU activity overlaps with human trafficking abuses aboard fishing vessels and also within communities that service the fishing vessels in port. The coincidence of these activities indicates that these problems are related, and are being driven by the global demand for fish and fish products.

There is a significant variation of compliance and enforcement, as with many issues, within national fishing fleets, with the U.S. fleet generally considered highly compliant with domestic and international laws, while others, such as Thailand have a poor record, implicated in cases of illegal fishing, human trafficking abuses, and human smuggling. Despite the high compliance rates within the U.S. fleet, illegal fishing by foreign vessels poses problems for the United States, particularly along the U.S.-Mexico border where there has been a drastic increase in recent years in the number of incursions of illegal Mexican fishing vessels called "lanchas" into U.S. waters. Local U.S. Coast Guard officials describe these illegal Mexican fishing vessels as a "persistent challenge to U.S. sovereignty,"[20] and recent reports suggest that these same vessels are also used to smuggle drugs and humans from northeast Mexico into Texas.[21] Likewise, small boats that would typically be used for fishing are a common mode of transport for undocumented migrants attempting to enter the United States, using California beaches as a landing point. Smugglers are paid up to $9,000 per person for these dangerous voyages that often end in deaths.[22]

Human trafficking in particular is a complex, international problem that must be addressed through a variety of legal and diplomatic channels. Once entered into force, the Port State Measures Agreement will strengthen port inspections, enhance communications, and deny port entry—including port services and supplies—to suspected illegal fishing vessels. The PSMA is a cost-effective enforcement mechanism that will begin to change the economic incentives—increasing the cost associated with illegal fishing because it will be more difficult for illegal vessels to access global markets. Once a suspected illegal fishing vessel is identified, countries will coordinate enforcement efforts to ensure that the suspected vessel is refused entry at other ports until the vessel agrees to be inspected or is prosecuted. The increased accountability and economic incentives in the PSMA could help to erode other criminal activities that are often associated with illegal fishing, including human trafficking. Currently, the European Union and 8 other nations have ratified the agreement, and 25 nations must ratify for the instrument to go into force. The world is waiting for the United States to act, and many nations will undoubtedly follow.

In 2000, Congress enacted the Trafficking Victims Protection Act which defined trafficking for the purposes of labor or sex and provided critical measures to protect human trafficking victims. This law was reauthorized for the fourth time in March 2013 with bipartisan support as strong as I witnessed as a staff member of this committee in 2000. The Port State Measures Agreement in particular complements this widely supported law, and institutes standards that are consistent with existing U.S. practice, and could pay big dividends globally through enhanced accountability, monitoring, communication, and enforcement of suspect fishing vessels that may be engaged in human trafficking or other criminal activities. The Port States Measures Agreement provides a pathway to beginning to address the complicated problem of human trafficking on the high seas. I strongly urge the U.S. Senate to demonstrate leadership and immediately ratify and implement the Port State Measures Agreement, sending a message to the world that we will not tolerate illegal fishing and its associated human rights violations.

A 2009 peer-reviewed scientific study estimated that the worldwide annual value of losses from illegal and unreported fishing could reach $23.5 billion.[23] Yet, vessels engaged in illegal, unregulated fishing not only steal precious food resources off the coasts of poor countries and damage marine ecosystems. They engage in drug smuggling. Most serious, they also prey on human beings. Illicit fishing worldwide appears to be rife with human trafficking. All the treaties and agreements under consideration at this hearing would regularize and shed sunshine on that fishing.

As a result they would not only prove more stewardly for marine econsystems, and more fair to businesses playing by the rules—as reflected by my fellow panelists—but helpful to prevent vulnerable people from being utterly dehumanized, violated, and even killed in that illicit fishing.

End Notes

[1] U.S. Department of State. (2013). ''Trafficking in Persons Report—June 2013.'' See http://www.state.gov/j/tip/rls/tiprpt/2013/.

[2] See http://notmylife.org/fishing-boys-lake-volta.

[3] See http://news.msn.co.nz/nationalnews/8767033/nz-goes-to-interpol-over-rogue-trawler.

[4] Dyck, A.J. and Sumaila, U.R. (2010). ''Economic Impact of Ocean Fish Populations in the Global Fishery.'' Journal of Bioeconomics, DOI: 10.1007/s10818-010-9088-3.

[5] United Nations Office on Drugs and Crime (UNODC). ''Transnational Organized Crime in the Fishing Industry—Focus on: Trafficking in Persons, Smuggling of Migrants, and Illicit Drugs Trafficking.'' (2011). See http://www.unodc.org/documents/human-trafficking/IssuelPaperl-lTOClinlthelFishinglIndustry.pdf.

[6] Skinner, E. Benjamin. (February 23, 2012). ''The Fishing Industry's Cruelest Catch,'' Bloomberg Businessweek. See http://www.businessweek.com/printer/articles/22538-the-fishing-industrys-cruelest-catch.

[7] International Organization for Migration (IOM). (2011). Trafficking of Fishermen in Thailand. See https://www.iom.int/jahia/webdav/shared/shared/mainsite/activities/countries/docs/thailand/Trafficking-of-Fishermen-Thailand.pdf.

[8] Service, Shannon, and Palmstrom, Becky. (June 19, 2012). ''Confined to a Thai Fishing Boat, For Three Years.'' NPR. See http://www.npr.org/2012/06/19/155045295/confined-to-a-thai-fishing-boat-for-three-years.

[9] United Nations Inter-Agency Project on Human Trafficking (UNIAP). (2009). ''Exploitation of Cambodian Men at Sea.'' See http://www.no-trafficking.org/reportsldocs/siren/sirenlcb3.pdf.

[10] International Organization for Migration (IOM). (2011). ''Trafficking of Fishermen in Thailand.'' See https://www.iom.int/jahia/webdav/shared/shared/mainsite/activities/countries/docs/thailand/Trafficking-of-Fishermen-Thailand.pdf.

[11] Environmental Justice Foundation. (2013). ''Sold to the Sea—Human Trafficking in Thailand's Fishing Industry.''See http://ejfoundation.org/sites/default/files/public/SoldltolthelSealreportllo-res-v2.pdf.

[12] Ibid.

[13] U.S. Department of State. (2013). Trafficking in Persons Report—June 2013. See http://www.state.gov/j/tip/rls/tiprpt/2013/.

[14] Ibid.

[15] Voice of America. (July 19, 2013). ''Sierra Leone: Government Targets Human Trafficking.'' Voice of America. See http://allafrica.com/stories/201307200024.html.

[16] U.S. Department of State. (2012). International Narcotics Control Strategy Report (INCSR). See http://www.state.gov/j/inl/rls/nrcrpt/2012/vol1/184098.htm.

[17] United Nations Office on Drugs and Crime (UNODC). (2011). Transnational Organized Crime in the Fishing Industry—Focus on: Trafficking in Persons, Smuggling of Migrants, and Illicit Drugs Trafficking. See http://www.unodc.org/documents/human-trafficking/IssuelPaperl-lTOClinlthelFishinglIndustry.pdf.

[18] Asian-Pacific Economic Cooperation Fisheries Working Group. (2008). ''Assessment of Impacts of Illegal, Unreported and Unregulated (IUU) Fishing in the Asia-Pacific.'' APEC Singapore. See http://www.imcsnet.org/imcs/docs/apecl2008liuulfishinglassessmtlselasia.pdf.

[19] United Nations Food and Agriculture Organization (FAO). (2007) ''Fishing Capacity Management and IUU Fishing in Asia.'' Bangkok.

[20] Mendoza, Jesse. (September 6, 2013). ''U.S. Coast Guard Seizes 1,000 Pounds of Illegally Caught Fish.'' Valley Morning Star. See http://www.valleymorningstar.com/news/locallnews/articlela1a39b6a-1772-11e3-a961-001a4bcf6878.html.

[21] Tompkins, Shannon. (June 11, 2013). ''Gulf Poachers Threaten to deplete Fisheries.'' Houston Chronicle. See http://www.houstonchronicle.com/sports/outdoors/article/Gulf-poachers-threaten-to-deplete-fisheries-4589290.php.

[22] Carcamo, Cindy. (September 14, 2012). ''For Illegal Immigrants, Ocean is the New Desert.'' Orange County Register. See http://www.ocregister.com/articles/san-371399-people-smuggling.html.

[23] Agnew, David J., et al. (February 25, 2009). ''Estimating the Worldwide Extent of Illegal Fishing.'' PLOS ONE. See http://www.plosone.org/article/info:doi/10.1371/journal.pone.0004570.

Senator MARKEY. Beautiful. Thank you, Mr. Ambassador. Now we will hear from you, Mr. Gleason.

STATEMENT OF MARK GLEASON, EXECUTIVE DIRECTOR, ALASKA BERING SEA CRABBERS, SEATTLE, WA

Mr. GLEASON. Good afternoon, Mr. Markey and members—well, no members of the committee. Thank you for the opportunity to testify at today's hearing. My name is Mark Gleason and I am the executive director of the Alaska Bering Sea Crabbers. We are a Seattle-based trade association representing 70 percent of the crab fishermen in the Bering Sea. Our members are small independently owned family businesses providing living wage jobs to thousands of Americans. These jobs include not just fishing jobs, but also jobs in the seafood processing sector, transportation and logistics, restaurant workers, and those in the retail trade. We brave the waters of the Bering Sea to produce the highest quality crab for our domestic and international customers.

I am here today, like the other panelists, to discuss the issue of illegal, unreported, and unregulated fishing. As you have heard, globally the IUU seafood trade results in economic losses of between $10 and $23 billion annually. Here in the United States, the Bering Sea crab fishery illustrates a prime example of what can happen to the market when it is flooded with IUU product.

In 2011, the Alaskan fishery brought in roughly 80 million pounds of live crab. The official Russian harvest in that year was about 91 million pounds. However, upon further examination of Russian trade data it appears that Russia actually exported closer to 189 million pounds in 2011. This 98-million-pound discrepancy can certainly be attributed to IUU production. Not surprisingly, in Alaska we experienced a 25-percent decline in the price we received for our crab as this pulse of illegal Russian crab entered not only the United States market, but the global supply chain as well.

Unfortunately, 2011 was not unique. A recent article in the Wall Street Journal noted that illegal Russian crab on the world market increased by an additional 36 percent between 2011 and 2012. That same article cited statistics from NOAA indicating that illegal Russian crab has cost U.S. fishermen $560 million since 2000. As you heard from Senator Murkowski, this also cost Alaskan coastal communities millions in lost tax revenue. Clearly, we must take action to prevent further harm to U.S. fishermen and fishing-dependent coastal communities.

As a globally traded seafood commodity, the supply chain for Russian crab from the point of harvest to the point of consumption is exceedingly complex. Initially the crab is harvested illegally in Russian waters by vessels flying flags of convenience. Although these vessels are not flying the Russian flag, they are oftentimes crewed and controlled by Russian nationals, in violation of Russian law.

The crab is then offloaded to transport vessels at sea. This practice is known as transshipment. These transshipment vessels then deliver the crab to ports in either Japan or South Korea, where it is processed and integrated into the supply chain. Along the way there are multiple opportunities to obscure the origin of this illegal product, either through misrepresentation involving fraudulent paperwork or by commingling the illegal product with legal product. This makes it nearly impossible for the end user to distinguish between legally and illegally caught crab. This illegal supply chain is driven by highly motivated and sophisticated international criminal conspiracies operating in multiple countries.

My association is under no illusion that there is a single silver bullet that will remedy this situation. We understand that it will take a combination of intergovernmental cooperation, private sector initiatives in both the United States and Russia, and a robust regulatory regime with adequate enforcement capacity to put a dent in this illicit trade.

Operating under the assumption that all seafood products must eventually come to port, the Agreement on Port State Measures is a major achievement in the global fight against IUU. This agreement requires nations to effectively police their ports and ensure that illegally harvested seafood products are not able to enter global trade. The United States was a leader in drafting this agreement. In order for us to continue to demonstrate our leadership, we must act now to ratify the agreement and then pass domestic legislation to fully implement the agreement here at home.

I urge the committee to take the first step and report this agreement favorably.

The Bering Sea crab fishery is a recognized model for sustainability. The fishery is prosecuted under stringent scientifically informed catch limits. Our fishing gear is environmentally sensitive and has a minimal impact on the sea floor. We have a transparent management process guided by science and stakeholder involvement. We have spent considerable time and effort to fully develop our markets, both here and abroad. We are proud of the product we bring to market and we welcome fair competition.

But the playing field must be level. As long as illegal Russian crab is afforded unfettered access to the world market, the playing field will not be level.

The agreement before you today is a significant step in the right direction. The choice is clear. We can support U.S. fishermen and coastal communities or we can continue to allow pirates and international criminals to profit from the illicit trade in IUU Russian crab.

[The prepared statement of Mr. Gleason follows:]

PREPARED STATEMENT OF MARK H. GLEASON

Good afternoon, Mr. Chairman and members of the committee. Thank you for the opportunity to testify at today's hearing. My name is Mark Gleason and I am the Executive Director of the Alaska Bering Sea Crabbers. We are a Seattle-based trade association representing 70 percent of the crab fishermen in the Bering Sea. Our members are small, independently owned family businesses providing living wage jobs to thousands of Americans. These jobs include not just fishing jobs, but also jobs in the seafood processing sector, transportation and logistics, restaurant workers and those in the retail trade. We brave the waters of the Bering Sea to produce the highest quality crab for our domestic and international customers.

I am here today to discuss the issue of Illegal, Unreported, and Unregulated fishing. For the remainder of my testimony I will refer to this as "IUU." Globally the IUU seafood trade results in economic losses of between $10–$23 billion annually.[1]

Here in the U.S., the Bering Sea crab fishery illustrates a prime example of what can happen to the market when it is flooded with IUU product. In 2011 the Alaskan fishery brought roughly 80 million pounds of live crab to market. The "official" Russian harvest was about 91 million pounds that year. However, upon further examination of Russian trade data, it appears that Russia actually exported closer to 189 million pounds in 2011. This 98 million pound discrepancy is attributed to IUU production. Not surprisingly, in Alaska we experienced a 25 percent decline in the price we received for our crab as this pulse of illegal Russian crab entered not only the U.S. market, but the global supply chain as well.

[1] Agnew DJ, Pearce J, Pramod G, Peatman T, Watson R, et al. (2009) "Estimating the Worldwide Extent of Illegal Fishing." PLoS ONE 4(2); e4570.

Unfortunately, 2011 was not unique. A recent article in the Wall Street Journal [2] noted that illegal Russian crab on the world market increased by an additional 36 percent between 2011 and 2012. That same article cited statistics from the National Oceanic and Atmospheric Administration indicating that illegal Russian crab has cost U.S. fishermen $560 million since 2000. Alaskan coastal communities have also lost out on roughly $11 million in tax revenue during this same period. Clearly we must take action to prevent further harm to U.S. fishermen and fishing dependent coastal communities.

As a globally traded seafood commodity, the supply chain for Russian crab from the point of harvest to the point of consumption is exceedingly complex. Initially, the crab is illegally harvested in Russian waters by vessels flying what are known as "flags of convenience." Cambodia and Sierra Leone are two of the most common flags of convenience. Although these vessels are not flying the Russian flag, they are often times crewed and controlled by Russian nationals, in violation of Russian law. The crab is then off-loaded to transport vessels at sea. This practice is known as transshipment. These transshipment vessels then deliver the crab to ports in either Japan or South Korea where it is processed and integrated into the supply chain. Along the way there are multiple opportunities to obscure the origin of this illegal product either through misrepresentation involving fraudulent paperwork or by comingling the illegal product with legal product. This makes it nearly impossible for the end user to distinguish between legally and illegally caught crab. This illegal supply chain is driven by highly motivated and sophisticated international criminal conspiracies operating in multiple countries.

My association is under no illusion that there is a single "silver bullet" that will remedy this situation. We understand it will take a combination of intergovernmental cooperation, private sector initiatives in both the U.S. and Russia, and a robust regulatory regime with adequate enforcement capacity to put a dent in this illicit trade.

Operating under the assumption that all seafood products must eventually come to port, the Agreement on Port State Measures to Prevent, Deter, and Eliminate Illegal, Unreported, and Unregulated Fishing is a major achievement in the global fight against IUU. This Agreement requires Nations to effectively police their ports and ensure that illegally harvested seafood products are not able to enter global trade. The United States was a leader in drafting this Agreement. In order for us to continue to demonstrate our leadership we must act now to ratify the Agreement and then pass domestic legislation to fully implement the Agreement here at home. I urge the committee to take the first step and report this Agreement favorably.

The Bering Sea crab fishery is a recognized model for sustainability. The fishery is prosecuted under stringent, scientifically informed catch limits. Our fishing gear is environmentally sensitive and has a minimal impact on the seafloor. We have a transparent management process guided by science and stakeholder involvement. We have spent considerable time and effort to fully develop our markets, both here and abroad. We are proud of the product we bring to market and welcome fair competition. But the playing field must be level. As long as illegal Russian crab is afforded unfettered access to the world market, the playing field will not be level. The Agreement before you today is a significant step in the right direction. The choice is clear. We can support U.S. fishermen and coastal communities or we can continue to allow pirates and international criminals to profit from the illicit trade in IUU Russian crab.

Thank you once again for the opportunity to testify and I would be happy to answer any questions.

Senator MARKEY. Thank you, Mr. Gleason, very much.

Captain Kane, you testified about your extensive experience as a fishermen. In your experience, do American fishermen engage in illegal fishing?

Mr. KANE. You know, Senator, as constrained as all U.S. fisheries have become, as you well know, you always get a couple of bad apples in the barrel, but over the years, with National Marine Fisheries, electronic vessel trip reports, vessel monitoring systems—think of 1984, satellites in the sky—we know where our boats are. So, as I said, you might get a couple of bad apples.

Senator MARKEY. You are saying compliance, though.

---

[2] Carlton, Jim. "Alaska Crabbers Get Pinched by Poachers." Wall Street Journal. 3 April 2013.

Mr. KANE. Yes. Yes, over the years National Marine Fisheries, NOAA, Coast Guard, we have gotten much better compliance here in the States.

Senator MARKEY. So you are saying it is a vast difference between out on the open sea in terms of enforcement of illegal fishing?

Mr. KANE. Well, there is no enforcement on the open sea, Senator.

Senator MARKEY. I know that. I am trying to make it—it is a leading question in the courtroom. I am trying to give you an opening.

Mr. KANE. Okay. Well, you know, take for example Cape Cod. You only have so many ports where you can land and enforcement is standing at the dock, whether it be State enforcement, Coast Guard, Federal enforcement. That is why I believe with foreign fishing vessels coming into the Nation you need stated ports where they have to call in before they land so you can send an inspection team down there to inspect cargo.

Senator MARKEY. To you, Mr. Gleason. You testified about the economic impact of illegal fishing on fishermen in your region. How will the Port State Measures Agreement help mitigate that problem?

Mr. GLEASON. Well, as other folks have testified, it will raise the cost of doing business for pirate fishermen, reducing the economic incentives and hopefully reducing the supply that is available on the market.

Senator MARKEY. Captain Kane, how will it impact yours?

Mr. KANE. Our fishing?

Senator MARKEY. How does the impact of illegal fishing affect your industry and how will this agreement help to mitigate the problems?

Mr. KANE. Well, for instance, bluefin tuna, which is a precious and desired fish in Japan, you have got a lot of piracy going on on the high seas, fish being shipped directly to Japan, and we are in convention—as the gentleman from NOAA was speaking about ICCAT, the International Commission for the Conservation of Atlantic Tuna, and if we can eliminate the high piracy at sea our fishermen will benefit in price on the Japanese market.

Senator MARKEY. What kind of benefits would American fishermen receive? What does it mean financially to them?

Mr. KANE. Well, first and foremost, you would save the species, because undocumented fish—once again, Senator, bad numbers into a computer model, no matter how many sensitivity runs you make you are going to get bad data out, and then management has to make decisions. So if you do not know what is being taken from the ocean, first and foremost the sustainability of the stock, that particular stock.

If you could stop the piracy—once again, it is supply and demand on the fresh Japanese fish market. Fewer fish on the market, tattooed fish, allocated fish, fish that we know were taken from the high seas, legal fish, will return a better price.

Senator MARKEY. Ambassador Lagon, can you discuss the role that international governmental communication plays in combating human trafficking and what role the Port State Measures Agreement could play in increasing that communication?

Ambassador LAGON Thanks for the question. Human trafficking is fundamentally a human rights issue. But to the degree that it is a law enforcement issue, the increased capacity of nations to communicate with each other about patterns makes great sense. The PSMA and the other agreements that the Senate Foreign Relations Committee are looking at would facilitate the ability of states to share information when there is a tip, including the ability of a flag state of a vessel to talk to a port state. This business of now essentially leaving the regulation of vessels entirely to the flag state, not being able to catch them where it would be easiest to spot—in ports—would be ameliorated.

All sorts of examples of human trafficking that I saw in the State Department role I played from 2007 to 2009 involve cooperation between law enforcement, immigration officials, and others. So the treaties will shine a light on this this problem and better permit that coordination.

Senator MARKEY. You testified that there is a governance black hole. As we heard in the testimony today, participation in regional fisheries organizations like the ones under consideration today increase governance and law enforcement presence on the high seas. In your work have you come across a connection between organizations like these and reductions in illegal fishing, human trafficking, other criminal activities such as that which you described in your testimony?

Ambassador LAGON Well, the empirical data on the extent of human trafficking is as hard to pin down as the data on the extent of illegal fishing. But these regional organizations and the commissions that have been created by the three regional agreements will facilitate an enforcement capacity of nations. I think one of the best bargains is, in fact, the technical assistance they would give to smaller, poorer states to be able to develop that capacity. That is a pretty small investment for the United States to make in something that will serve the interests of business, serve the interests of preserving biodiversity, and especially serve the goal of being able to catch people who would enslave other human beings at sea.

Senator MARKEY. Let me finish up the hearing this way. Let me give each one of you, in reverse order of recognition for the opening statement, an opportunity to just tell us the key thing, couple of things, you want this committee to remember, you want the Senate to remember as we consider whether or not to ratify these treaties. So we will begin with you, Mr. Gleason.

Mr. GLEASON. Well, as I mentioned in my testimony, I represent many hardworking American fishermen and we provide jobs up and down the supply chain. We play by the rules. We are fully engaged in the management process. We support the science that goes into that. We play by the rules, and we just want a level playing field. The Port State Measures Agreement will help to get us that level playing field.

Senator MARKEY. Thank you, Mr. Gleason.

Ambassador.

Ambassador LAGON Thank you. As far as human trafficking goes and how these agreements and the PSMA would affect it, there are two key messages, I believe. First, human trafficking is always about some group of people—women, children, migrants, people of less privileged castes in India—not having access to justice. In these areas where there is a grey zone, where there is no governance, where there are no eyes monitoring, those people who may have rights on paper, in treaties, or in laws, are not getting protected. These agreements would help with that.

Then secondly, human trafficking is about bad people, transnational criminals, having an incentive of profit and very little risk. The PSMA in particular would change that incentive structure, would make it more economically costly for people to pursue IUU fishing and in turn costly to be able to pursue forced labor or even sexual exploitation, by removing this "black hole" of governance.

Senator MARKEY. Thank you.

Mr. Kane.

Mr. KANE. I can sum it up in probably three: It would be good for U.S. fishermen, east coast, west coast, nationally; it would be good for the fish stocks, all these fish we are trying to save so we can fish them at a sustainable rate; it would be good for the United States monetarily.

Senator MARKEY. Thank you, and we thank each of you. I would like to wrap up the hearing by reiterating a statement that Captain Kane has in his written testimony: "Fishermen feel the double whammy of the fish, that we abstain from harvesting to ensure a sustainable stock, are harvested through illegal fishing, and yet when we do harvest our quota the markets and prices for our fish are depressed because of the presence of that illegal catch in the marketplace."

So I think that we have our work cut out for us, but I think it is imperative that we pass this treaty, that we pass all the treaties, and we do so this year, and we send a signal to the world, we send a signal to all of these pirates, all of these criminals, that finally the United States is going to be a cop on the beat enforcing these laws. Finally, we are going to be protecting our fishermen and protecting these species. I think it is imperative that, going forth from this committee today, that they hear this message and get ready for these treaties to be ratified.

We thank each one of you for your testimony. We thank you for your work on this issue. The record will remain open until February 21 for additional information to be included within it.

With that, this hearing is adjourned. Thank you.

[Whereupon, at 4:19 p.m., the hearing was adjourned.]

ADDITIONAL MATERIAL SUBMITTED FOR THE RECORD

RESPONSE OF DEPUTY ASSISTANT SECRETARY DAVID BALTON TO QUESTION SUBMITTED BY SENATOR ROBERT MENENDEZ

Question. What is the administration's position on whether the four agreements considered at the hearing on February 12, 2014, are self-executing in the United States?

Answer. It is the administration's position that none of the four agreements considered at the hearing on February 12, 2014, are self-executing.

RESPONSES OF DEPUTY ASSISTANT SECRETARY DAVID BALTON TO QUESTIONS
SUBMITTED BY SENATOR MARCO RUBIO

Question. If the U.S. ratifies the South Pacific Convention, what is our estimated budget obligation?

Answer. Under current conditions, the U.S. assessed contribution to the South Pacific Regional Fisheries Management Organization is estimated at $65,000 annually. Exact costs are variable, based on the overall budget level of the Commission, foreign exchange rates, and the extent of U.S. catches in the Convention Area.

Question. In your testimony you state that the Northwest Atlantic Convention Amendments under consideration would reduce the U.S. budgetary contributions by one-third.

♦ Do you have an exact estimate of the amount that would be due?
♦ Would this increase the contributions of other countries and, if so, do you fore-see other convention countries opposing this amendment?

Answer. Our current assessed contribution to NAFO is approximately $295K annually. Costs are variable based on foreign exchange rates and the level of U.S. catches but, under current conditions, this would be reduced to approximately $200K.

Yes, this would increase the contributions of other nations accordingly, but the increased cost would be spread across the other 11 members of the Commission. The amended budget formula corrects a recognized and unintended anomaly that resulted in the overcounting of U.S. harvest for the purposes of the budget calculation. As a result, all members of the Commission have supported this amendment without objection.

Question. In your testimony you describe other illegal activities which are often intertwined with illegal, unreported, unregulated fishing (IUU) including organized crime and labor exploitation but fail to name human trafficking. There have been numerous report of human trafficking has been linked to IUU fishing.

♦ Can you go into more detail about how the tools of the IUU Agreement will com-bat organized crime, labor exploitation, and human trafficking?

Answer. The Port State Measures Agreement will help combat IUU fishing and the associated activities identified above in a number of ways. First and foremost, the agreement will establish new rules and requirements for vessels entering the ports of States party to the agreement, provide heightened authority for port inspec-tors to board and inspect fishing vessels entering their ports, and allow them to deny entry into ports for vessels identified as having engaged in IUU fishing. Collec-tively, the measures will make it easier to detect and take action against such ac-tivities, raise the costs to those engaged in illegal activities, and take some of these vessels off the water. To be clear, the agreement is focused on combating IUU fish-ing, but to the extent that it constrains this illegal activity, it will have ancillary benefits in these other areas.

Question. As you know, Cuba and China are Contracting Parties to the South Pacific Convention. Under the Convention's Article 19, Contracting Parties must cooperate with developing Contracting Parties by providing:

i. Financial assistance;
ii. Technical assistance relating to human resources development;
iii. Technical assistance;
iv. Transfer of technology; and
v. Advisory and consultative services.

♦ What are the implications of Art. 19 of this Convention with respect to U.S. pol-icy on Cuba? What are the implications of Art. 19 with respect to U.S. policy on China?

Answer. Article 19 will not result in any change in U.S. policy with respect either to Cuba or China. Among other things, Article 19 notes that, "in giving effect to the duty to cooperate, . . . members of the Commission shall take into account the spe-cial requirements of developing coastal State Contracting Parties in the region, *in particular, the least developed among them and small island developing States* (emphasis added).

To the extent the U.S. becomes a party to the Convention, it would not hamper our ability to adhere to all existing provisions of law prohibiting assistance to Cuba.

China, which is Party to other fisheries Conventions with similar provisions, has never sought any of this kind of assistance for itself, and we would not expect it to do so under the South Pacific Convention. More important Article 19(4) is clear that cooperation activities "may include" provision of the types of assistance listed in the question above, but creates no obligation on any Party to do so.

Question. How does U.S. ratification of any of these Conventions affect current U.S. policy regarding UNCLOS?

Answer. U.S. ratification of these Conventions will not affect current United States policy regarding the Law of the Sea Convention. The United States is already a Party to several regional fisheries management organizations for which the underlying Conventions contain provisions comparable to those in the current agreements.

Question. Can the U.S. indefinitely and effectively protect its interests and discharge its obligations under any of these Conventions without ratification of UNCLOS?

Answer. As noted in the previous response, the United States is a Party to several regional fisheries management organizations whose underlying Conventions contain provisions based on the same principles as the four agreements currently pending before the Senate. U.S. ratification of the Law of the Sea Convention would strengthen our ability to advance U.S. objectives in a wide range of areas, but would not prevent us from protecting U.S. interests and discharging our obligations under these four Conventions.

RESPONSES OF RUSSELL SMITH III TO QUESTIONS
SUBMITTED BY SENATOR MARCO RUBIO

Question. In your testimony, you state that the minimum standards set by Port States Agreement track closely to what the United States already does. What are the differences between current U.S. standards and the Port States Agreement's minimum standards?

Answer. The minimum standards for the training of inspectors and conduct of inspections contained in the Port State Measures Agreement, once broadly implemented, will have a significant impact on the global effort to combat illegal, unreported, and unregulated (IUU) fishing. Those minimum standards were drafted with significant participation from NOAA and the U.S. Coast Guard, and they are consistent with current U.S. practice.

Apart from the establishment of minimum standards for inspections, the most significant binding obligation in the Port State Measures Agreement is the obligations to deny listed IUU fishing vessels port entry unless they are being allowed to enter for the purpose of inspection or enforcement. When this obligation is implemented NOAA anticipates an active role, along with the U.S. Coast Guard, in the screening of vessels seeking entry into U.S. ports to assess their listed status or, for vessels that are not included on a Regional Fishery Management Organization's IUU vessel list, respond to evidence of IUU fishing or activities in support of IUU fishing. Specifically, the U.S. Coast Guard and NOAA will continue to improve cooperation on the Advance Notice of Arrival process for foreign vessels entering U.S. ports for the purposes of implementing the agreement and the two agencies have already had discussions on developing the needed level of collaboration in order to carry out the requirements of restricting port access when needed.

Question. What budgetary impacts, if any, will result from NOAA's implementation of the Port States Agreement as the primary agency? Does this in any way expand NOAA's role beyond activities already being conducted at the agency?

Answer. NOAA is not seeking specific funding increases to carry out its responsibilities in the agreement beyond what has been included to support a broader array of international enforcement activities in the FY 2015 Budget request.

As discussed above, NOAA will have an increased role in coordinating with the U.S. Coast Guard on the evaluation of foreign fishing vessels seeking entry to U.S. ports to determine if there is evidence of IUU fishing or support of IUU fishing. NOAA will also have an increased role, again in coordination with the U.S. Coast Guard, in restricting access to port services for IUU fishing vessels detected within a U.S. port.

Finally, the Port State Measures Agreement has information-sharing requirements that require the sharing of inspection results and actions taken with flag states, relevant coastal states, Regional Fishery Management Organizations and other relevant international bodies. This will be a new process that will require NOAA to develop a communications mechanism to share the information.

Question. Do you anticipate any additional economic burden at ports in the United States as a result of the Port States Agreement?

Answer. Because there are a relatively small number of known IUU fishing vessels, and only two such vessels have ever entered a U.S. port, impacts are likely to be negligible. However, there could be negative economic impacts on U.S. companies providing port services as a result of lost business if a fishing vessel is denied port entry or access to port services. There may also be some costs to state, local and territorial authorities in coordinating with NOAA to implement the obligations under the Port States Measures Agreement regarding the denial of access to port services to IUU fishing vessels determined to be in a U.S. port.

For example, the Port State Measures Agreement creates the potential to avoid economic loss from a repeat of the Polestar situation in which $9 million of sustainably caught Pollock from Alaska was denied port entry in the European Union and Morocco because it was carried on an IUU fishing-listed cargo vessel that had come into port in Dutch Harbor, AK, because NOAA didn't have the authority to deny the IUU fishing-listed cargo vessel port entry.

Question. A common theme we hear from fishermen as we work to reauthorize the Magnuson-Stevens Act is the economic hardships they experience when their days on the water are limited due to factors beyond their control. How will these agreements help address that issue?

Answer. The North Pacific and South Pacific Conventions, the Northwest Atlantic Fisheries Organization Convention Amendment and the Port State Measures Agreement will not have an immediate impact on fisheries management within the U.S. Exclusive Economic Zone. These agreements will provide the United States new tools to improve global fisheries governance and management that will ultimately benefit U.S. fishers and others working in the fisheries sector by raising the standards applied to foreign fishers and markets to those already applied in the United States. The Port State Measures Agreement does not regulate any fishing at sea but, by requiring parties to conduct some level of port inspections, provides a mechanism for monitoring compliance with conservation and management measures adopted by coastal states and regional fisheries management organizations.

We have no fishers operating at present in the Convention Areas of either the North Pacific Convention or the South Pacific Convention. We do have one fishing vessel that operated in the Northwest Atlantic Fisheries Organization Convention Area in 2012 and 2013, and two fishing vessels have applied to fish in 2014. The Northwest Atlantic Fisheries Organization does not regulate fisheries by limiting days at sea. Rather, it establishes a total allowable catch for a fish stock and then allocates national quotas to its members from the total amount. Thus, the Northwest Atlantic Fisheries Organization does not regulate fisheries through effort controls such as a limit on days at sea.

RESPONSES OF ADM. FREDERICK J. KENNEY TO QUESTIONS
SUBMITTED BY SENATOR MARCO RUBIO

Question. With the ratifications of the four treaties, the "Northwest Atlantic Fisheries Organization" Convention, the "North Pacific" and "South Pacific" Conventions, and the "Port State Measures" Agreement, what specific steps would the Coast Guard be able to take to combat Illegal, Unregulated, and Unreported (IUU) fishing?

Answer. General.—International mechanisms, such as these four treaties, strengthen governance over fishing activity on the high seas assist the Coast Guard by extending authority to board and inspect fishing vessels covered by the relevant Convention. Boardings increase maritime domain awareness and act to deter illicit behavior through fear of being caught.

NAFO Amendment.—Under the NAFO Amendments the Coast Guard will continue to facilitate joint boardings/inspections with Canadian Department of Fisheries and Oceans officials as opportunities present. These compliance inspections will help to discourage IUU fishing in the North Atlantic and ensure the U.S. is meeting enforcement obligations under the Convention.

Port State Measures.—Port State Measures will facilitate close coordination between NOAA and the Coast Guard to stem IUU fishing activities. These measures will deny access to U.S. ports by vessels engaged in IUU fishing except for the exclusive purpose of conducting inspections or engaging in other enforcement activities. While the implementing legislation seeks to provide NOAA organic authority to deny port access, the Coast Guard will be instrumental in facilitating U.S. actions. This may include providing advance notice of arrival information, tracking vessels of interest or assisting with boardings. Without access to ports, vessels engaged in IUU fishing will not be able to sell their product or receive logistical support for operations. This will force these vessels into ports farther from commerce centers and lucrative fishing grounds, and, as a result, will likely increase their operating costs. Limiting the ports available to these vessels would simplify enforcement by targeting investigations of illicit activity in ports known to support IUU fishing.

North and South Pacific RFMOs.—The Coast Guard will work with partners at Department of State and NOAA to ensure the inclusion of robust boarding and inspection procedures within both the North and South Pacific Regional Fisheries Management Organizations that will increase opportunities to board and inspect fishing vessels on the high seas, throughout the Pacific Ocean. The establishment of a governance scheme in this remote region provides oversight of fishing activity in an area not previously covered. The Coast Guard will leverage available patrol assets and, to the extent practical, utilize naval vessels of opportunity through the Oceana Maritime Security Initiative (OMSI) to track and board fishing vessels to combat IUU fishing.

Question. If the Coast Guard boards a ship which is suspected of IUU and finds evidence of human trafficking, what steps can the Coast Guard take?

Answer. The Coast Guard team will investigate, collect evidence, and report their findings through the chain-of-command to interagency partners, including the Department of State, Department of Justice, and other applicable U.S. agencies in accordance with the Maritime Operational Threat Response (MOTR) plan. The flag state of the vessel has exclusive jurisdiction over offenses committed on board. If the vessel is flagged in the United States or is a vessel without nationality, the Coast Guard could seize the vessel and coordinate with the Department of Justice for prosecution of the offender under domestic human trafficking laws. If the vessel is foreign-flagged, jurisdiction to seize and prosecute would have to be coordinated with the flag state; exceptions include foreign flagged vessels located within the U.S. territorial sea or the offense is committed by a U.S. national or person with status in the U.S. Exercising jurisdiction over a U.S person on board a foreign flagged ship on the high seas would still involve consultation with interagency partners through the MOTR process. Interagency consultation provides the ability to determine whether the United States has an independent basis to exercise jurisdiction (e.g., the vessel is in the U.S. territorial sea, it is a U.S. vessel or a vessel without nationality, or the offender is a U.S. national) or whether the matter will be referred to the vessel's cognizant Flag State for action based on exclusive flag state jurisdiction over its vessels.

Question. With the ratification of these treaties, would the Coast Guard need additional resources or personnel to assist with U.S compliance?

Answer. Ratification of these four treaties will not require the Coast Guard to seek additional resources or personnel to ensure U.S. compliance. Enforcement of these treaties will primarily be conducted as part of existing efforts on the high seas and outer reaches of the U.S. Economic Exclusive Zone (EEZ) by Coast Guard offshore patrol assets.

————

RESPONSES OF AMBASSADOR MARK LAGON TO QUESTIONS
SUBMITTED BY SENATOR MARCO RUBIO

Question. What current work is being done by the U.S. Government to combat human trafficking on fishing vessels?

Answer. The U.S. Coast Guard and National Oceanic and Atmospheric Administration (NOAA) show an acute awareness of criminal and inhumane activities in fishing on the high seas, as reflected in their testimony in the hearing. For this reason, they join the State Department in endorsing the ratification of the Port States Measures Agreement, the Conventions on the North and South Pacific Fisheries Resources, and the Amendment to the Northwest Atlantic Fisheries Convention the hearing addresses—legal instruments the State Department helped negotiate.

As I spoke to in my written testimony, the Department of State's Office to Monitor and Combat Trafficking in Persons (TIP) under my leadership from 2007 to 2009 and that of the estimable Ambassador CdeBaca since 2009, have increasingly focused on human trafficking in the fishing sector. In my testimony, I highlight how Thailand represents a special hazard zone for human trafficking in illegal fishing. Well, during my tenure it became apparent that human trafficking was flourishing in the seafood processing sector on Thailand's soil; I met female victims from Myanmar in person near Samut Sakhon. I surprised my fellow Republicans by standing with the leader of the Solidarity Center, the AFL–CIO affiliated democracy-promotion organization funded by the National Endowment for Democracy, at the public release of their report on forced labor in the seafood sectors of Thailand and Bangladesh. The TIP Office between 2007 and 2009 also helped highlight boys trafficked in fishing in the Great Lakes of Africa. Ambassador CdeBaca's team has taken this focus on fishing farther, including that on the high seas, as seen in annual "Trafficking in Persons (TIP) Reports" in his tenure.

By highlighting this issue in the TIP Report, in what happens to be the most successful public diplomacy instrument in the State Department's toolbox today, thanks to the Congress handing the Department that tool, the concern of states about what I call in my testimony "governance black holes" has increased. The TIP Report is just the beginning of the TIP Office's work, as it is followed by quiet, intense diplomacy to urge governments to take the steps needed to objectively merit a higher ranking. What the U.S. urges in that diplomacy is plainly spelled out in a paragraph labeled "Recommendations" in each country profile in the TIP Report. As important as this public and traditional diplomacy is the assistance the U.S. gives to NGOs and international organization agencies to build nations' will and capacity to fight trafficking.

Trafficking on the high seas is not so easy to combat, nor to underwrite the work of NGOs and international organizations to combat, absent treaties placing more responsibility on port states and also of to-date rather hands-off flagging states of fishing vessels. U.S. public and traditional diplomacy has boosted the potential for international support for these treaties. U.S. ratification would be an even more powerful symbolic measure to encourage other nations to become parties, and in the most important case of the PSMA, allow it to reach the threshold of parties needed to come into force.

Question. Your testimony highlights a few countries which have had evidence of human trafficking in the illegal fishing industry.

♦ Are there certain hot spots for this specific type of trafficking?

Answer. The Conventions on the North and South Pacific Fisheries Resources, as two instruments the hearing addresses, highlight two such hot spots. My testimony alludes to a Korean vessel in Northeast Asia. Yet, the South Pacific and the region nearby Southeast Asia are particularly problematic. This is the reason for special focus in my written testimony on Thailand, and the trafficking of Thai, Cambodian, and Burmese workers. (And please note that Thailand this year faces the time limit on a Tier 2 Watch List ranking under the Trafficking Victims Protection Act as amended in 2009, just as Russia, China, and Uzbekistan did last year. Thailand would be a worthy focus of the committee's oversight this spring and summer.) The combination of economic desperation, migrant workers' ambitions to send remittances back to their family, corruption, greedy ship proprietors sneaking into other nations' territorial waters, and the ungoverned space of the high seas make Southeast Asia a breeding ground for netting people for slavery as well as netting sealife with no regard for sustainability.

Another large region with pronounced problems is the African Continent. I have spoken of boys fishing on Lake Volta. But beyond inland bodies of water, off the shores of much of western and eastern Africa, thriving corruption and piracy and lacking governance and monitoring make them hot spots too.

It is important to recall that much of the fishing industry is decent and above-board, as represented by those testifying beside me. It is for this very reason that those playing by the rules ought not have their reputations and competitiveness undercut by illicit fishing vessels who also dehumanize fisherman.

♦ Is there a "typical" type of trafficking victim for this crime?

Answer. There are three categories of "targets" for human trafficking: (1) migrant workers who are undocumented, and through force, fraud, and coercion become victims; (2) migrant workers who are legal guest workers lied to about the work they will get, purposefully put deeply into debt, and relieved of their passport and papers; and (3) those victimized in their own nation or by their own nationals. It was a priority of my time as Ambassador at Large to Combat Trafficking in Persons that the Office I supervised would call attention to just how much of human trafficking counterintuitively is in the latter two categories.

Human trafficking in legal fishing appears to occur most in Group #1 and Group #3. U.N. Office on Drugs and Crime (UNODC), International Organization for Migration (IOM) and press reports I highlight in my testimony give an accounting of exploited workers desperate for better lives for themselves and their families, but just risk-taking enough to be lured into illegal fishing. Some cases involve fisherman being violently exploited by nationals of their own country.

Most significant in the profile of a ''typical'' victim are (1) his or her needs and dreams to which a trafficker appeals, (2) methods of recruitment, and (3) means of exploitation and abuse.

First, the victims are impoverished, and willing to take on dirty and dangerous work in order to make a living for themselves and relatives.

Second, unregulated recruiters lie about the pay, safety of the fishing conditions, legality of standards and location of fishing, and the ability to leave the job.

Third, exploitation sometimes involves debt bondage (an insurmountable debt owed to a recruiter or to the fishing ''enterprise'' for the privilege of being placed in work which will amount to forced labor). Victims interviewed in Southeast Asia note being caught on boats unmonitored by any law enforcement or labor inspectors for up to 2–3 years, excruciating hours, lack of medical care, ill fisherman thrown overboard, and punitive beatings and even murder.

If the treaties this hearing addresses could shed sunlight on this ungoverned zone, and even marginally reduce this dehumanization, it is well worth the minimal cost to the United States to ratify them. I surmise they will actually do a good amount to reduce this dehumanization.

LETTER SUBMITTED ON BEHALF OF THE FEDERAL
LAW ENFORCEMENT OFFICERS ASSOCIATION

FEDERAL LAW ENFORCEMENT OFFICERS ASSOCIATION
1100 Connecticut Ave, NW, Suite 900
Washington, DC 20036
(202) 293-1550

Representing Members Of:
AGRICULTURE-OIG and FOREST SERVICE
COMMERCE
  Export Enforcement, OIG
  & NOAA Fisheries Law Enforcement
DEFENSE
  Air Force - OSI
  Army - CID
  Defense Criminal Investigative Service
  Naval Criminal Investigative Service
  OIG
EDUCATION - OIG
ENERGY
  National Nuclear Security Adm
  OIG
ENVIRONMENTAL PROTECTION AGENCY - CID & OIG
FEDERAL DEPOSIT INSURANCE CORPORATION - OIG
GENERAL SERVICES ADMIN -OIG
HEALTH & HUMAN SERVICES
  Food & Drug Administration & OIG
HOMELAND SECURITY
  Border Patrol
  Coast Guard Investigative Service
  Immigration & Customs Enforcement
  Customs &Border Protection
  Federal Air Marshal
  Federal Emergency Management Agency
  Federal Protective Service
  US Secret Service
  Transportation Security Administration
  OIG
HOUSING & URBAN DEVELOPMENT - OIG
INTERIOR
  Bureau of Indian Affairs
  Bureau of Land Management
  Fish & Wildlife Service
  National Park Service
  OIG
  U.S. Park Police
JUSTICE
  Bureau of Alcohol, Tobacco, Firearms & Explosives
  Drug Enforcement Administration
  Federal Bureau of Investigation
  US Marshals Service
  OIG
U.S. Attorney's Office-CI
LABOR- OIG & Racketeering
POSTAL SERVICE
  Postal Inspection
  Postal OIG
SOCIAL SECURITY ADMINISTRATION - OIG
STATE DEPARTMENT
  Bureau of Diplomatic Security & OIG
TRANSPORTATION-OIG
TREASURY
  FINCEN & OIG
  Internal Revenue Service - CI
  TIGTA
U.S.CAPITOL POLICE
U.S. PROBATION & PRE-TRIAL SERVICES
VETERANS AFFAIRS - OIG
RETIREES

NATIONAL OFFICERS

President
  JON ADLER
Executive Vice President
  NATHAN CATURA
Vice President - Operations
  LARRY COSME
Vice President – Agency Affairs
  CHRISTIAN SCHOPPMEYER
Vice President – Membership Benefits
  JOHN RAMSEY
Secretary
  ENID FEBUS
Treasurer
  KURTIS ROINESTAD
Vice President-Legislative Affairs
  FRANK TERRERI
National Chapters Director
  ROB SNYDER
National Awards Director
  CHRISTINA HONEYWELL
National Recruitment Director
  RASHEED TAHIR
General Counsel
  LAWRENCE BERGER
Public Information Officer
  JENNIFER MATTINGLEY

February 7, 2014

The Honorable Robert Menendez
Chairman
U.S. Senate Committee on Foreign Relations
446 Dirksen Senate Office Building
Washington, DC 20510

Dear Chairman Menendez:

On behalf of the Federal Law Enforcement Officers Association (FLEOA), the largest nonprofit professional association representing 26,000 current and retired federal law enforcement officers across the nation, including member NOAA special agents and uniformed officers, we write to express our strong support for the International Fisheries Stewardship and Enforcement Act (SB 269/HR 69), the Pirate Fishing Elimination Act (SB 267), and the Port State Measures Agreement. We urge you to immediately pass these important bills to enhance domestic and international enforcement efforts to protect our valuable fisheries resources for law-abiding U.S. fisherman and our coastal communities.

The U.S. Coast Guard (USCG) and the National Oceanic Atmospheric Administration's, Office for Fisheries Law Enforcement (NOAA OLE) are responsible for protecting living marine resources within the U.S. Exclusive Economic Zone (EEZ), including preventing foreign illegal fishing and supporting international efforts to eliminate fisheries-related crime on the high seas. In addition, enforcement activities often transcend fisheries crime, as foreign illegal fishing vessels are known to engage in other types of transnational crimes, including drug and human trafficking, posing a persistent challenge to U.S. sovereignty.

Immediate passage of SB 269/HR 69; SB 267 and the Port State Measures Agreement would simplify enforcement protocols and provide the U.S. Coast Guard and the NOAA Fisheries service, Office for Law Enforcement additional tools to improve enforcement, enhance port security, protect our law enforcement officers, and take stronger action against foreign illegal fishing operators.

Specifically the International Fisheries Stewardship and Enforcement Act (IFSEA) would harmonize existing enforcement protocols and establish streamlined standards for taking action against foreign illegal fishing vessels. The legislation also increases officer safety by making it an explicit violation to assault or otherwise oppose law enforcement officers in the enforcement of existing international fisheries laws. Finally, SB 269/HR 69 would enhance cooperation between the U.S. Coast Guard, NOAA OLE, other law enforcement partners, the Department of Defense and increase the resources available to enforcement officers to detect, track and prosecute foreign illegal fishing activity.

The Pirate Fishing Elimination Act would implement the Port State Measures Agreement, an international treaty that would close ports around the globe to foreign vessels engaged in illegal fishing, eliminating pathways for illegal product to enter the global fish market and reducing the economic incentive for foreign illegal fishing operators. Passage of this bill would encourage other nations to meet U.S. Standards by implementing common-sense port inspection and control requirements resulting in a broad increase in overall maritime security.

Passage of SB 269/ HR 69; SB 267 and ratification of the Port State Measures Agreement will enable U.S. law enforcement officers to more safely and effectively apprehend foreign illegal fishing operators and build on domestic and international efforts to eliminate fisheries-related crime. Please pass these important measures as soon as possible.

Sincerely,

Jon Adler

Jon Adler
FLEOA National President

JA/CJS

LETTER SUBMITTED ON BEHALF OF THE JOINT OCEAN COMMISSION INITIATIVE

The Joint Ocean
Commission Initiative
Leadership Council

Co-Chairs

The Honorable
William Ruckelshaus
The Honorable
Norman Mineta

Members

Frances Beinecke

The Honorable
Samuel Bodman, Ph.D.

Donald Boesch, Ph.D.

Lillian Borrone

The Honorable
Norman Dicks

Vice Admiral
Paul Gaffney,
U.S. Navy (Retired)

Robert Gagosian, Ph.D.

Sherri Goodman

Scott Gudes

Paul Kelly

Vice Admiral
Conrad Lautenbacher, Ph.D.
U.S. Navy (Retired)

Margaret Leinen, Ph.D.

Christopher Lischewski

The Honorable
Jane Lubchenco, Ph.D.

Julie Packard

John Pappalardo

The Honorable Leon Panetta

The Honorable
Pietro Parravano

Diane Regas

Andrew Rosenberg, Ph.D.

Patten White

JOINT OCEAN COMMISSION INITIATIVE

February 11, 2014

The Honorable Harry Reid
Majority Leader, United States Senate
522 Hart Senate Office Building
Washington, DC 20510

The Honorable Mitch McConnell
Minority Leader, United States Senate
317 Russell Senate Office Building
Washington, DC 20510

Dear Majority Leader Reid and Minority Leader McConnell:

On behalf of the Joint Ocean Commission Initiative, a collaborative, bipartisan effort to catalyze ocean policy reform, we strongly encourage ratification of four international fisheries treaties currently before the Senate Committee on Foreign Relations:

- Agreement on Port State Measures to Prevent, Deter, and Eliminate Illegal, Unreported and Unregulated Fishing (Port States Measures Agreement on IUU);
- Convention on the Conservation and Management of High Seas Fisheries Resources in the North Pacific Ocean (North Pacific Convention);
- Convention on the Conservation and Management of High Seas Fishery Resources in the South Pacific Ocean (South Pacific Convention); and
- Amendment to the Convention on Future Multilateral Cooperation in the Northwest Atlantic Fisheries (Northwest Atlantic Convention Amendment).

In furthering recommendations from the Pew Oceans Commission and the U.S. Commission on Ocean Policy, the Joint Initiative has long supported policies for the conservation, sustainable use, and ecosystem-based management of living marine resources.

The U.S. Commission on Ocean Policy's landmark report, *An Ocean Blueprint for the 21st Century*, noted that "the effective management and conservation of global marine species, and the enforcement of international treaties, require a combination of domestic, bilateral, regional and international approaches. Although regulation of fisheries on the high seas is conducted within broad regions of the seas, the existing regional fishery organizations are generally weak. They lack adequate resources or enforcement capabilities…"

The Port State Measures Agreement on IUU, along with legislation to implement it (S.267, The Pirate Fishing Elimination Act), would directly address a major threat to sustainable management and stewardship of global fishery resources: illegal, unregulated and unreported (IUU) fishing. This agreement is designed to help ensure that illegally harvested fish do not enter international commerce, which has significant adverse impacts on the U.S. fishing industry and U.S. fishermen by depleting global fish stocks and introducing unfair competition on the global seafood market.

Illegally harvested fish that enter the U.S. also have an adverse effect on the regulatory agencies responsible for monitoring, regulating, and enforcing U.S. fisheries policies by skewing the critical data that the agencies, especially the Fishery Management Councils, use in modeling fish stocks and assessments for sustainable utilization. Using the premise that all fish caught commercially at sea must be landed at a port, the Port State Measures Agreement on IUU would require party nations to take a number of steps to combat IUU activity, including denying port entry and access to port services to foreign fishing and transport vessels that have harvested fish illegally.

The South Pacific Convention, North Pacific Convention, and Northwest Atlantic Convention Amendment establish and/or strengthen regional fisheries management organizations (RFMOs) "to ensure the long-term conservation and sustainable use of the fisheries resources in the Convention Area."

Sustainable management of our ocean resources for current and future generations requires an international framework and a consistently applied rule of law across nations. Ratification of these treaties, taken as a whole, is an important step in this direction and helps affirm the role of the United States as a leader in protecting our global commons for the benefit and use of our citizens.

Sincerely,

William Ruckelshaus
Co-Chair, Joint Ocean Commission Initiative

Norman Mineta
Co-Chair, Joint Ocean Commission Initiative

LETTER SUBMITTED ON BEHALF OF VARIOUS STAKEHOLDERS
URGING RATIFICATION OF THE TREATIES

February 10, 2014

The Honorable Harry Reid
Senate Majority Leader
United States Senate
Washington, DC 20510

The Honorable John Boehner
Speaker of the House
U.S. House of Representatives
Washington, DC 20515

The Honorable Mitch McConnell
Senate Minority Leader
United States Senate
Washington, DC 20510

The Honorable Nancy Pelosi
House Minority Leader
U.S. House of Representatives
Washington, DC 20515

Dear Senator Reid, Speaker Boehner, Senator McConnell, and Representative Pelosi:

We represent a diverse group of stakeholders that share a common interest in healthy U.S. fisheries that support a robust domestic seafood industry and vibrant coastal communities. We are writing to urge you to support and quickly pass the International Fisheries Stewardship and Enforcement Act (S. 269/ H.R. 69) and the Pirate Fishing Elimination Act (S. 267) and to ratify the Port State Measures Agreement (Agreement). These bipartisan bills and the agreement would improve enforcement of illegal fishing on the high seas, keep suspected foreign illegal fishers out of U.S. ports, and protect U.S. fishermen, our domestic seafood supply, and the global health of our oceans from the damage wrought by pervasive unlawful fishing.

According to the National Marine Fisheries Service (NMFS), the domestic seafood industry, which includes harvesters, seafood processors, dealers, wholesalers and retailers, generated $52 billion in sales impacts and supported more than 786,000 jobs in 2011. We are very concerned about the impacts of foreign illegal fishing activity on U.S. economic interests. Illegal, unreported, and unregulated fishing accounts for up to 26 million tonnes of fish annually – six times more fish than the entire U.S. commercial fishing industry catches every year. Foreign illegal fishing on the high seas could impact the U.S. fishing industry by depleting global fish stocks and introducing unfair competition on the global seafood market.

In addition to economic impacts, recent reports demonstrate a clear link between foreign illegal fishing vessels and other types of transnational crime, including human trafficking, smuggling of illicit drugs, and illegal immigration. On April 18, 2013, for example, the Coast Guard seized 2,200 pounds – $27 million dollars' worth – of cocaine that was headed to the U.S. on a fishing vessel in the Western Caribbean. The U.S. State Department's 2013 International Narcotics Control Strategy Report indicates that foreign fishing vessels are a common mode of transport for illegal drugs.

Finally, illegal fishing puts the law-abiding U.S. fleet at risk of reduced quotas and more restrictive management measures. Many internationally managed stocks that migrate between the U.S. EEZ and the high seas have become overfished due to foreign illegal fishing, such as Atlantic Bluefin tuna. Between 2008 and 2011, quotas for Atlantic Bluefin tuna in the Mediterranean were exceeded by 77% due to foreign illegal and unreported fishing. This illegal fishing undermines internationally-agreed upon quotas, and the decline in global fish populations due to illegal fishing means U.S. fishing fleets must expend more resources in pursuit of a dwindling population of wild fish.

We respectfully request your support to pass the Port State Measures Agreement and the two pieces of legislation to strengthen U.S. enforcement capabilities, keep foreign illegal fishing vessels out of U.S. ports, and send a strong signal that the U.S. stands firm behind the U.S. seafood industry, coastal communities, consumers and sustainable fisheries.

Thank you in advance for your urgent attention to this issue.

Sincerely,

ALBION FISHERIES LTD.
Guy Dean, Vice President - Import/Export CSO

AT SEA PROCESSORS ASSOCIATION
Stephanie Madsen, Executive Director

AUSTRALIS AQUACULTURE LLC
Josh Goldman, Co-Founder & CEO

BI-RITE MARKET
Sam Mogannam, Owner

CALIFORNIA AQUACULTURE ASSOCIATION
Michael Lee, Executive Director

ENVIRONMENTAL JUSTICE FOUNDATION
Steve Trent, Executive Director

FISHWISE
Tobias Aguirre, Executive Director

FORTUNE FISH CO.
Mark Palicki, Vice President of Marketing

GREENPEACE USA
John Hocevar, Oceans Campaign Director

LUSAMERICA FISH
Fernando Frederico, President

MONTEREY BAY AQUARIUM
Aimee David, Ocean Conservation Policy Director

NEW ENGLAND AQUARIUM
Meghan Jeans, Director of Conservation

OCEANA
Corry Westbrook, Federal Policy Director

PASSMORE RANCH
Michael Passmore, President

SANTA MONICA SEAFOOD
Logan Kock, Vice President of Strategic Purchasing & Responsible Sourcing

SEACORE SEAFOOD INC.
Sal Battaglia, Director of Operations

SEA DELIGHT
Cesar Bencosme, Vice President

SEA PACT
Logan Kock, Board Chairman

SEATTLE FISH CO.
Derek Figueroa, Chief Operating Officer

SHEDD AQUARIUM
Michelle Parker, Vice President, Great Lakes and Sustainability

TATAKI SUSHI BARS
Raymond Ho, Chef & Founder
Kim Lui, Chef & Founder
Casson Trenor, Sustainability Expert & Founder
Kenny Zhu, Chef & Owner

WORLD WILDLIFE FUND
Roberta Elias, Deputy Director, Marine and Fisheries Policy

Cc:
The Honorable John Rockefeller, Chairman
U.S. Senate Commerce Committee

The Honorable John Thune, Ranking Member
U.S. Senate Commerce Committee

The Honorable Doc Hastings, Chairman
House Natural Resources Committee

The Honorable Peter DeFazio, Ranking Member
House Natural Resources Committee

The Honorable Robert Menendez, Chairman
U.S. Senate Committee on Foreign Relations

The Honorable Bob Corker, Ranking Member
U.S. Senate Committee on Foreign Relations